Dog Scooter

The Sport for Dogs Who Love to Run

by Daphne Lewis

Dog Scooter
The Sport for Dogs Who Love to Run

Copyright 2005 Daphne Lewis

All rights reserved. Except for brief quotations, no part of this book may be reproduced in any manner whatsoever without prior written permission from the publishers.

ISBN: 1-4116-5706-3
ISBN-13: 978-1-4116-5706-9

Cover photos courtesy of Filip Chudil, Czech Republic.

Photo of author on sulky courtesy of Lourdes Laurente, Big Pixel Studio.

Text and photos by author unless otherwise noted.

Cover and interior book design by Gregory Banks (BDDesign) for Lulu.com

Printed & Published by LuLu.com

To the warm hearted and open-minded people on the e-mail talk group **"DogsLovetoRun@yahoogroups.com"** who have continually educated me since the group began in 2000.

"I believe that 99.99% of all dogs in the US are made to do something they don't want to do, every day: sit around the house until they die, doing absolutely nothing.

Thank God for the people who give their dogs work to do that they love and live for.

I think Dog Scootering is a lot more important than any of us knows."

Joseph Brown, Seattle, Washington

November 21, 2004

Contents

Introduction i

Why Teach Your Dog to Pull a Scooter? 1

    Dog and you have fun 1

    Dog and you become working partners 2

    Dog and you become fit 3

    Dog scootering is easy and inexpensive 4

    Train your lead dog 6

    Hyper dogs calm down 6

Don't Walk The Dog!!! by Victoria Rose 8

History 11

What Breed of Dog? 17

    Characteristics of a good scooter dog 19

Equipment 22

    Harness 22

    Tug line 25

    Scooter 27

    Dog 30

    Additional Equipment and Supplies 31

Dog Health & Safety 33

Training the Dog to Pull a Scooter 37

    Commands 37

    Manners 39

    Training 40

    Conditioning 55

    Coaching 58

How will the sport develop? 62

Acknowledgments

As someone who has owned and trained fewer dogs than practically any scooterer I know, I owe my ability to write this book to other people's ideas, advice and expertise. Tim White encouraged me in 1997 to promote the sport of dog scootering. My friend, Cheryl Reehill, has over and over again answered questions on the DogsLovetoRun e-mail list. I have eagerly read these electronic words and listened closely to her in-person advice to me. Cheryl's training ideas have become my ideas. Many of the ideas in this book are ones I absorbed from her. Jill Miller of Michigan gave me the DogScooter logo and hosted scooter races in Michigan. Seattle mushers, Carmen Rasmussen and Becky Loveless of Alpine Outfitters, encouraged me and supported my efforts to promote scootering. They designed harnesses for scootering, hosted Fun Runs, organized work shops and tirelessly answered questions. Megan Capon has never failed to answer my questions or review my work with prompt answers based on experience and thought. I thank you all.

Introduction

Leash laws make the city more civilized, but force new problems on our generation of dog owners. It's an easy problem to pick up your dog's poop from city sidewalks and to keep your dog off your neighbor's porch. It is a big problem to exercise a creature who loves to run faster than you can and to zig and zag when by law, he must walk in a straight line on a leash at a human pace. If you work eight hours a day, you walk the dog around the block before and after work and before going to bed. This is not enough exercise for a middle or large size dog and it bores you. It is one more chore, like taking out the garbage.

Dog owners are resourceful. They jog with their dogs. They roller blade with them. They take their dogs to day care. They bicycle with their dogs. They would throw dummies into the water for their dogs to retrieve, but Seattle does not allow dogs into the water! Seattle has salt water Puget Sound along its west edge and fresh water Lake Washington along its east edge. Are dogs dirtier and do they poop in water more than seals and salmon, ducks and Canada geese?

Dog owners have to deal with Animal Control. Once I decided to roller blade with my dog around Green Lake, a distance of 2.8 miles on a paved pathway. Mindful of the danger of overheating, I threw a dummy into the Lake to cool him down before we started our run. Rubro swam straight for the dummy ignoring ducks. As he was swimming straight back towards me dummy in mouth, obviously under control, Animal Control showed up - two men on bicycles. They called headquarters and found out that Rubro indeed had a license. Two counts against me: dog off leash, dog in a city lake. Could have been three counts had Rubro been unlicensed. The fine was $70.

In 1996 the Seattle Parks Department built trial dog parks in large open areas in eight different parks. The trial dog parks were popular. Those that became permanent are used consistently and intensely. Dog parks are used more heavily and more consistently than any other section of park. Even on rainy days, the rare snowy days, Sunday mornings, and Christmas, dogs and their owners are at the dog parks.

Leash laws created the need for these dog parks. At the parks the dogs run free, socialize with other dogs, and fetch frisbees and tennis balls. They provide a safe place to run dogs off leash. But there are problems. Dog parks are overcrowded and tend to be muddy. Getting to the park is inconvenient. Most people need to drive the dog to the park rather than just walk across the street. Most importantly, though, dog parks are dangerous. Dogs bully other dogs, especially small dogs. Bullied dogs become fearful and even dog aggressive. In addition there is the human need to move about. I don't much like standing around refereeing dogs. I'd rather be scootering down a trail.

And so I bought a harness and a scooter and hitched Rubro to it. A new sport! Dog Scootering!

Why Teach Your Dog to Pull a Scooter?

Dog and you have fun.

Dogs love to run. At dog class the instructor told us to walk faster if the dogs seem bored. Moving faster cheers them up, energizes them. The instructor set up jumps. The dogs got to run and jump the jumps. The energy in the room doubled. In 2004, my little pit bull, Millie, gave a scooter demonstration at a pet expo. We were given a 20 by 50 foot enclosed area for our demonstration. There was no trail to follow. How were we going to show spectators the thrill of scootering in that little space? How were we going to have our dogs RUN from one end of the demo area to the other. The night before the demonstration, we put bits of hot dogs at each end of the demo area. We ran Millie on leash from end to end a few times to get the hot dogs. She learned to run the length of the 50 foot demo area in a straight line. During the actual demonstration there were no hot dog rewards. Millie enjoyed <u>running</u>. She picked up speed as she ran; she opened her wide pit bull mouth and smiled as she pulled her scooter at a run past the audience. The running was her reward. She was having fun running and I was having fun riding the scooter and smiling at her enjoyment.

Scooter dogs get excited when the harness comes out. The harness means it is time to run. Some scooter dogs drag their harnesses to their humans or even their humans to their harness when they want to go. Some scooter dogs woo-woo - or bark, or growl or jump with excitement - when their harness comes out. Some owners try to sneak harness and scooter to car without their dogs seeing it. They want to avoid the noise of excitement. Scootering is fun for dog and human from the very first runs. Recently I helped a man teach his dog to pull her scooter. My Millie became the rabbit that his malamute chased. The malamute pulling her scooter chased Millie pulling her scooter. We went a short distance for a short amount of time. We stopped before the malamute got tired even though both of us were having fun and wanted to keep going. It is hard to stop scootering even when you know it is wise to do so.

Scootering becomes more fun as the dog and you become more proficient and you can go farther and faster. Dog scootering becomes addictive. When Rubromarginata, my rottweiler, was young, we scootered after I got home from work. We scootered to the grocery store and post office. We scootered to and through city parks. On weekends we drove out of town and spent two or three hours exploring new trails and large regional parks. Books about rail trails and mountain bike trails became my bed time companions and exploring the beautiful Washington woodlands became my addiction.

Dog and you become working partners.

"How do you steer the dog?" The answer to this question is one of the most addictive parts of dog scootering. The dog thinks; and that is how you steer him. You watch and admire his thinking. For example Rubro and I used to go to woodland parks on a Sunday morning. After two hours of climbing and descending hills and choosing various paths, I would decide it was time to return to the car --- only I was lost! Where is the car? "Rubro, go to the car!" And I rode the scooter and Rubro steered and pulled. He always knew which path would get us back to the car. We were working partners. In this instance he was the thinking partner; I was the scooter managing partner. More typical examples of you-don't-steer-the-dog are the constant small decisions the dog makes on the trail. "This part of the trail is more comfortable, so we are running here not there." The dog makes these decisions; you don't.

One of my favorite examples of "you don't steer the dog" is the trained scooter dog pulling his scooter in a city park. Rubro is trotting along Bluff Trail. A dog walking on a leash approaches making body language of "Let's say Hi". Rubro ignores the dog and passes the dog without veering and without me saying "On by". I did not steer him. He made the proper trail decision himself.

Of course many times you do steer the dog. There is a fork in the trail. The dog sees the fork. You see his ears perk up asking which way to go. You say, "Rubro, gee", and he takes the right hand

---

CJ Schuler of Woodland, California, explains via e-mail to a questioner in 2004 that indeed dogs enjoy scootering.

LOL!!!! He's welcome to come watch when I get mine ready to go run. Eli starts running around the house "Woo-wooing" and nipping at me in his excitement. I have to trap him between my legs just so I can harness him. He's too excited to stand still. Then he'll see them run to the gate where the scooter and lines are. Eli is still bouncing around woo-wooing and biting the other dogs in play. Next you see Stache begin to quiver as he's hooked up. He and Makin' go right in to a good line-out because they know we won't move until they are lined out. Stache quivers in excitement until we take off. Eli gets hooked up and used to grab the line screaming to go. Now he has learned he has to settle before I'll go. Once I say "Let's Go", Stache starts talking and all three are running at full tilt.

I wouldn't do this if my dogs didn't enjoy it. Some days I don't feel like going out but I do because THEY want to! Most dogs enjoy the ability to run that fast and free. Show me another time when a dog can run for miles and miles like that. Even hiking for miles and miles with Makin doesn't afford her the freedom of running that scootering does. You could remind him that dogs work as a pack. The ability to function as a part of the team is something they understand. If he still isn't sure they enjoy the sport, he's welcome to try and carry one team dog while the others are running. It's like trying to hold on to a tornado. They don't just want to go along; they want to run!!!

None of my other dog activities gets this level of excitement from the dogs. They really don't.

* * * * *

Megan Capon, Cle Elum, Washington, also has dogs that are crazy to run. They love it. She writes in fall of 2004.

Now WHY do dogs love it so much? Shoot... In my opinion, it's another mystery right in there with "Why do dogs like rolling in aged road kill and eating horse poop?"

fork without changing pace. Other times you want the dog to cross an open field. Crossing a field is difficult because the dog does not have a path to follow. I say "This way!" and Rubro takes his cue from the direction the scooter is pointing. Trained leaders continue across an open space in a straight line - like a bird dog on a go-out to the bird.

"How do you steer the dog?" The dog thinks and that is how you steer him. My friend, Megan Capon, of Cle Elum, Washington, has german short hair pointers. These dogs hunt birds by preference but anything that moves including skunks and porcupines are prey and Megan must be alert. They scooter, skijor, cart, sled, and skateboard. They do these pulling sports at blinding speed. Once my friend had her "maniacs" on a forest service road pulling her four wheeled cart. They ran between two bollards. The cart caught because it was wider than the opening between the bollards. With the dogs charging into their harnesses, Megan, was unable to pull the cart and dogs backwards. Lead dog Dulcie backed up and pulled team mate Rogan backwards with her. This action released the pressure on the cart so that Megan could back it up. Dulcie then pushed Rogan to the wider opening on the other side of the bollard. The cart went through and the team was off and running. Dulcie understood the problem and solved the problem - in an instant! Why? Because she loves to run. Running is her reward for problem solving.

The other question is "How do you make him go?" The answer is "Going is what the dog wants to do". Mushers say, "You can't push a dog with a rope". What they mean is dogs run because they love to run. Scootering enables you to allow the dog to do what he loves to do.

You and the dog are a team.

Dog and you become fit.

You are the dog's teacher when you first start scootering. You teach the dog to pull in front of you and to follow commands. Once the dog "gets" it, you become his personal trainer and coach. You build his fitness and his skill. You gradually increase the length of the runs. You keep a log of time run and distance traveled. As the dog gets in better condition, he can maintain a sprint for longer intervals. He needs shorter rests between sprints. He can trot for more miles. He can change gait as requested by you - now faster, now slower.

Show dogs who scooter become hard muscled. They look great in the ring. They win ribbons. Hunting dogs who scooter have greater endurance in the field. Skijor dogs who scooter become fit before the snow flies. They are ready to win races.

1. Human competitors at a race in Szilvasvarad in Hungary run beside their scooters as they and their dogs rush up a grassy hill. The canine competitors run at human speed when going up hill. Photo courtesy of Filip Chludil of Czech Republic.

With a fit scooter dog you can explore miles and miles of trails. You look forward to long outings in faraway wild lands. Hurry up weekend.

The human also exercises when scootering with the dog. Millie, my 50 pound pit bull, was running eagerly along a rail trail. I was kicking hard to lighten her load so she could run faster. The more I kicked, the faster she ran. What fun! With my slow rottweiler I could not kick because if I did, the scooter would run into him. With him I liked to go on single track trails on hills. I ran beside the scooter when we went uphill. I got exercise also.

I kicked when we were on level but rough ground. I squeezed the brakes going downhill so as not to run into him and to keep the tugline tight. With both fast Millie and slow Rubro, I exercised when I scootered. I peeled off layers of clothing as we went along. For some people dog scootering means standing on the scooter and riding, especially people with multiple dogs. For me, with just one dog, dog scootering means exercising along with my dog.

Scooting without the dog is excellent aerobic exercise. Scoot as fast as you can for a half an hour. Kick in a rhythm. Stand on one leg and kick three times, then switch legs rhythmically. You will get an aerobic work out but you will not pound your knees the way a runner does. Then hitch up the dog for his turn, and fit is what you both will be.

2. Two golden retrievers lunge into their harnesses at the start of a scooter race in Washington State. The Northwest Sled Dog Club hosted the race in November, 2003. Sue Meinzinger, founder of Summit Assistance Dogs, is the driver. The two goldens are assistance dogs in her training program. The dogs are attached with a two-dog tug line. Photo by Linda von Hanneken-Martin.

Dog scootering is easy and inexpensive.

There are numerous sports for dogs. They vary from flyball to schutzhund, from hunting trials to frisbee, and from obedience to conformation. In addition there are the

by Daphne Lewis

pulling sports which include mushing, carting, cart driving, weight pull and scootering. All these sports tend to be more difficult and more expensive than dog scootering. To compete in agility you either need to buy or make equipment for your back yard or you must drive to a facility where the equipment is set up. To drive a sulky (driving) you need a sulky, harness and reins - and level areas to drive on.

Dog scootering is simpler. You need a harness, a tug line and a scooter. You can scooter in your neighborhood or you can drive to a trail in the outback. You can scooter at a leisurely trot or you can scooter at a full run. It depends on what you and your dog prefer.

3. A collie mix, an alaskan husky, and a whippet (known as the Motley Crew) enjoy scootering with owner musher Kathy Beaupre on a summer day in Ontario, Canada in 2003. The dogs are hitched abreast in a fan hitch. Photo by Liz Macfie's husband.

You can scooter with the dog you already own - assuming the dog is sound and weighs 25 pounds or more. Even Jack Russell size dogs can scooter as they do not need to provide all the power. With both small or large dogs, you must run beside the scooter to go up hills and to travel rough ground. Small dogs have less body mass and therefore dissipate heat better than large ones. Large dogs have longer legs and therefore cover ground with fewer strides. Both can pull a scooter! My friend, Cheryl Reehill, has a 40 pound black dog who is built like a mixture of whippet and cattle dog. That dog is crazy to run. She outruns the larger dogs in the household and comes back from 5 mile runs saying "That was nice, when do we get to run?"

For some dogs it makes sense to build up endurance for running 10 or 20 miles at a time. For others running a mile is enough. As long as the scootering is fun and the dog becomes fit, it does not matter whether you have a ground eating speed demon or a dog who enjoys shorter slower outings.

You can scooter with several dogs. Scootering is a wonderful way to exercise the family pack. Three 25 pound dogs will probably out-perform one 90 pound dog. Of course if you have endless energy pointers, three may be too much power and speed even for a large wheeled, heavy framed scooter.

Train your lead dog.

A dog scooter is an excellent tool for mushers to train leaders. Dogs that run with a team can be shy when run alone. The scooter lets them learn to run confidently by themselves - leading, thinking, pulling and running. Mushers can develop multiple leaders by working their dogs one at a time

Scootering is relaxing for the musher. Hooking up one or two dogs to a scooter is easy and recreational. There is not the raw, hard to manage power of a team of six to twenty hell-bent-to-go huskies.

Scootering allows older, slower dogs to run at their own speed. It allows young dogs to train to become leaders. Professional mushers hire handlers. The handlers need to learn how to handle a team. Hooking one or two dogs to a scooter allows the beginning handler to learn to mush.

Hyper dogs calm down.

Hyperactivity is a leading reason why dog owners surrender dogs to shelters. The Humane Society of St. Joseph, Indiana, interviewed 380 people who surrendered their dogs for adoption and 905 owners who kept their animals. Fifty-four percent of the dogs surrendered were six months to three years old and 15 percent were less than six months old. (The study did not include surrendered litters.) Behavior problems that contributed to surrender were:

- Barking, 41 percent
- Chewing, 24 percent
- Hyperactivity, 45 percent
- House training accidents, 21 percent
- Aggression to other pets, less than eight percent
- Aggression to people, less than nine percent

The first three problems are greatly reduced by ample exercise. In fact most hyperactive dogs are not hyper. They are under-exercised. Kim Tinker, champion skijorer and teacher of dog pulling in Oregon, says "There are no hyper dogs. There are exercise dependent dogs."

It is NORMAL for dogs, especially young dogs to need more than a half hour walk. In July, 2005, I hiked up a mountain with my cousin and my 9 month old presa canario, Tess. I hitched the leash to Tess' pulling harness and had her pull me up the mountain. The tugline never slacked. The hike lasted 5 1/2 hours. By the end of the hike, I had blisters on both my feet. The next two days my legs hurt. When we returned to the car, I took off Tess' saddlebags with their now empty water bottles and unleashed her. She immediately began running at top speed in large happy circles. We threw tennis balls for her and she retrieved them with energy.

Running and pulling a scooter is a great solution for exercising a dog. Dogs get plenty of hard, fun exercise in a reasonable amount of time. - more reasonable than a 5 1/2 hour hike up a mountain.

Don't Walk The Dog!!! by Victoria Rose

Why? Because walking does very little to fulfill a dog's exercise needs. Unless it's a VERY small dog (so that it has to run to keep up with you while you walk fast), walking on a leash is almost NO EXERCISE at all for a dog. Dogs must RUN to meet their exercise needs.

Few people realize how much exercise the average dog NEEDS. Lack of exercise (RUNNING at THEIR pace, not ours!) is the #1 reason too many dogs are hard to handle, out of control, and then end up either "driving" their owners "crazy," or worse, being turned over to shelters, usually because their owners decide they are "just too hyper."

Exercise is the most-neglected aspect of most dogs' lives and that which subsequently causes them, and their owners, the most grief.

As a rule: most dogs NEED to RUN (so walking on a leash is totally ineffective), until their energy is expended, 2x a day, RAIN OR SHINE, 365 days a year. Making sure they run is a chore, like feeding and grooming. It requires sacrifice on the part of the owner. Dogs need it for their own health and general well-being. They need it to relieve tension and to de-stress. Sadly, most owners neglect their dog's basic NEED for exercise. They may know the dog needs to get out and burn off some energy, but they feel too tired or too busy to meet this responsibility. They ignore (possibly because they are not aware of the importance of) their dog's basic need for exercise, even though that dog clearly is totally dependent upon them, and at their "mercy," for all its needs.

Just having a yard is not sufficient. Dogs generally do not exercise themselves in appropriate ways. If they are running, they are usually doing so in ways that disturb the neighbors and/or increase aggression, like barking or chasing children or other animals along the fence line.

The majority of dogs, especially those who get into trouble at home, are full of energy and under-exercised. They are the ones in the neighborhood barking at every little noise or activity they hear or see. These are the dogs chewing and digging up their yards. These are the dogs, that despite being social creatures, and REQUIRING social contact for their mental health, are relegated by unknowing or uncaring owners to the backyard – or worse, a chain - because they are deemed "too hyper" to be indoors.

First of all, it is wholly unfair to punish a dog because the consequence of our neglect annoys us. Secondly, there is no such thing as a hyper dog! There are only under-exercised (and untrained), dogs. These are the dogs whose basic needs are not being met, and for whom this (often-inadvertent) neglect is showing up as "behavior problems." (By the way – no one gets off the hook by saying their dog's behavior doesn't annoy them. Even if an owner has a high tolerance level, or a dog remains well-behaved, the dog still needs to run and exercise for his own mental and physical health.)

In dog training we say, "A TIRED dog is a GOOD dog." Properly-exercised dogs, as a rule, SLEEP ALL DAY. If a dog is awake and active all day, he probably is not getting enough exercise. I advise my students: "If you have time to either train your dog or regularly exercise your dog, get out of class now and set up a twice-daily exercise routine. Twice-daily exercise is much more important than training, and… a regularly exercised dog often doesn't even NEED any formal training because… a sleeping dog rarely gets into trouble and… 'A tired dog is a good dog.'"

These are a dog's BASIC NEEDS:

- Water
- Social companionship/living in the house with the family/playing with other dogs
- Exercise until "Hang Dog" tired twice a day, every day
- Mental stimulation (Training, getting out in public)
- Food (Good quality)
- Regular and emergency vet care (when needed – not waiting til payday)

Neglecting any one of these basic needs is to fail to meet the standards of responsible pet ownership.

A routinely, and well-exercised dog can tolerate an occasional shorter or missed session without much, if any, consequence. And older dogs or dogs with lower than average energy may do just fine on once a day – the proof is in their behavior. When running your dog, be aware that most will not simply just QUIT when sufficiently tired. They'll keep running. But if you take them home and feed them, you'll find them retiring to their beds to sleep. So you need to experiment to see how much exercise is enough for your dog. If you bring him home and feed him and he still bounces around the house, he probably didn't get enough.

Exercise requirement is one of the most important considerations when choosing a dog, and when making the effort to meet your responsibility for your dog's basic needs. It helps keep him out of trouble, makes him a better neighbor, and helps him to be easy to live with. And again – even if a dog whose exercise needs are neglected is not exhibiting bad behavior, he still is suffering mentally and physically from the lack of activity.

By the way: My breed, the Doberman pinscher, is a VERY high-energy breed. I have lived with them in my own homes on fenced-acreage, and in rented apartments with no yards, but my responsibility is the same either way: I take my dog some place where there is room to run first thing in the morning, and then again late afternoon or early evening. Each time, I throw the ball for her to retrieve or I let her run with other dogs or charge around chasing squirrel scent or I run her with the bike until she is pooped out. Mind you, I HATE this chore. I would much prefer to get up in the morning, shower, etc., and then work on the computer all day, but I LOVE having a dog and know that in order for one to be calm and relaxed enough to live peaceably in my home, and to follow my commands, I must meet her exercise needs. And because I choose to own a high-energy breed, I know I am required to be out there longer and/or more often than if I'd gotten a dog of a lower-energy breed. So choose your dog carefully. Choose one whose needs match what you are able and willing to offer.

Sometimes I "kill two birds with one stone" by taking projects with me to wherever I am going to run my dog. While supervising her, and in between throws of the ball, I can read a magazine, write a letter, look through my mail, sew on a button or organize my car.

Recently I took up Dog-Scootering. This sport is GREAT exercise (for Jetta) and FANTASTIC fun (for us both). She loves pulling me on the scooter and I love riding it. I have clocked her in the car at 25 mph. I think she has probably pulled me on the scooter at up to 20 mph. We whip along the trails at the local park... it's very exciting and she gets a terrific workout.

After she runs, we go home and I feed her, and she SLEEPS. My Doberman, like all my dogs before her, is always super-calm and super-relaxed due to the amount of exercise she gets each day. I do this every single day of the year, rain or shine, regardless of my busy schedule or lack of desire, because I recognize it as one of her basic NEEDS and one of my basic RESPONSIBILITIES. I would not neglect running my dog every day and every night any more than I would neglect feeding her. She is NEVER running around my house looking for things to do or reacting to neighborhood activity. My neighbors may not even know I have a dog. When she, like all my other dogs before her, is in the house (or apartment), she is quiet, "mellow," and ASLEEP.

Remember: A TIRED DOG IS A GOOD DOG.

BTW: Be aware you must not feed a dog, then exercise it. Always feed afterwards and after the dog has calmed down, to avoid bloat/torsion, which can be fatal. Also regulate water intake while exercising, and until he's calmed down, as this can also be a danger.

History

Dogs were working animals before they were pets. It is natural for a dog have a job. It is unnatural for a dog to sit around all day with nothing to do. Recently a coyote was radio tagged. In one week the coyote crossed three States and logged 800 miles. That is approximately the same travel schedule as Iditarod sled dogs, except the coyote took time out to hunt his own food.

The dog's first work for mankind was hunting - unless cleanup of camp sites by scavenging is work for mankind. If camp cleanup is work, then hunting was the dog's second job for mankind. Reproductions of Egyptian tomb paintings show dogs hunting. Soon after he mastered hunting, carrying and pulling gear became the dog's third job. Nineteenth century paintings of American Plains Indians show their dogs pulling gear on a travois. Dogs were draft animals for American Indians long before Spaniards introduced horses in the sixteenth century. Indians all over the continent had their preferred working dogs. A modern breed, the catahoula leopard dog, developed from dogs of the Choctaw Indians of Louisiana. The Choctaw dogs interbred with mastiffs of the invading Spaniards to become the present day catahoula leopard dog.

Herding became a job for dogs after people domesticated ungulates. Herding skills derive from hunting skills.

Each polar people developed dogs to hunt, haul, and herd: the eskimo dog of eastern Siberia, the Greenland/Inuit dog, the siberian husky and the samoyed dog of the Samoyeds of Siberia. The samoyed was especially versatile. He hunted walruses, guarded reindeer herds, and pulled sleds. His fur could be woven into clothing. The Alaskan malamute was developed by the Mahlemuts, an Inuit tribe who lived along the shores of Kotzebue Sound in the upper western part of Alaska. The malamute was bred for pulling a heavy sled in weather as cold as 50 Fahrenheit degrees below zero.

4. American Indians used dogs as draft animals during the centuries before the Spaniards brought horses to North America. Indian dogs hunted, hauled goods, played with the children, and slept in the tents. Etching courtesy of LaFlamme Farms, Selma, Oregon, breeders of American Plains Indian Dogs.

The chow chow of China was used for guarding junks and pulling carts - and for meals. "Chow" means "food".

Some European breeds were bred specifically for herding, hauling and carrying. The bouvier de Flandres was a farm dog for herding cattle, guarding the farm and pulling carts. Four Swiss mountain breeds were known as "the milkmen". These four, the appenzell mountain dog, bernese mountain dog, great swiss mountain dog, and the entlebucher sennenhund were used to haul cans of milk and mountain cheese from the stables to shops in town. When they were not drafting, they were on the farm herding livestock, playing with children and guarding the farm.

During the Alaska gold rush, St. Bernards, newfoundlands and any large dog with a good coat of fur could be shipped north to pull freight sleds. These dogs were mushing dogs because of the job they did, rather than because of their breed. "Although he is a superior water dog, the Newfoundland has been used and is still used in Newfoundland and Labrador as a working dog - dragging carts, or more, often carrying burdens as a pack horse[1]".

My point is that dogs evolved as working companions to man. The idea that it is cruel to give dogs work is a new one. I believe that asking dogs to do nothing but sit around the house or yard all day is unhealthy, boring, and unnatural. Even small dogs had jobs historically. Called turnspits, they walked in circles around the fire pit thus turning the meat. And terriers killed vermin.

Dog pulling has evolved since its beginnings 4,000 years ago. It came to modern attention during the Alaskan Gold Rush. Men who grew up working horses and mules flocked to Alaska and learned to haul freight with dogs. They called it mushing. Their dogs had to survive poor care and cold weather - and keep on pulling freight sleds. In the middle of the twentieth century, freight hauling dogs were replaced by trucks, airplanes, and snow mobiles. Dogs no longer delivered mail or hauled furs. Joe Redington, Sr. worried that a way of life in Alaska was fading from memory. It was important to keep the history of dogs in Alaska alive. Redington created the Iditarod race. The first race ran in 1973.

Mushing as recreation began at least as early as 1910 when the first races were held in Nome. When recreational mushers turned to racing, speed became more important than strength to break trail in deep snow and haul massive freight sleds. Mushers began crossing greyhounds, salukis and pointers with their huskies as early as 1910. The alaskan husky was developed and is developing. Its breed standard differs from others in that it is based on performance. A dog that can trot 50 to 100 miles a day or can sprint at 20 to 25 miles an hour for 20 miles is an Alaskan husky. A dog that can not do that is not.

---

[1] The Complete Dog book, 17th edition, The American Kennel Club, Macmillan Publishing Company, 1985, p.317.

by Daphne Lewis

5. Alaskan huskies love to run and have an upbeat, sensitive personality. Notice Ichiro's easy lope and the long reach of his front leg. Photo of Lourdes Laurente and Ichiro by her husband, Brad Sprague, Gig Harbor, Washington.

European mushers crossed European hunting dogs with Alaskan huskies. The new breed, called a eurohound by some and pointer crosses by others, looks more like a pointer than the traditional Alaskan husky. Eurohounds are sweeping the sprint racing circuit. Most pointer cross breeders agree that Alaskan huskies are as fast as eurohounds and pointers when running free. The pointer crosses maintain better speed than alaskan huskies while pulling as a team because of their heavier muscle mass and resistance to heat build up. Eurohounds are less popular in distance races because their coats are light. To run distance races with thin coated dogs, mushers must coat them, bootie them, feed them more calories, and give them straw to sleep on.

Dog scootering is mushing for the rest of us. It is for those who own one to a few dogs. It also is for mushers who want to train dogs individually. When did dog scootering begin? Perhaps it began when you as a kid put on your roller skates, hitched your leash to your doberman pinscher and took off down the sidewalk. Or maybe it began when your uncle was a teenager, put a harness on his pit bull, hopped on his skate board, and he and his pit bull roared around the lake at a gallop.

In Europe, New Zealand and Australia, dog scootering has been a sport since at least the 1980's. The first dry land sled dog race in New Zealand was in 1984 on the South Island.

Tim White is a mid-distance racer of international renown. In 1974 he was the first person to run the Iditarod from outside Alaska. He won the Yellowknife Canadian Championship 6 times, beginning in 1977. He has raced on four continents and is known worldwide as a goodwill ambassador for the sport of mushing. Often he goes abroad as race marshall for important races, ie., large purse races. Tim wrote in an e-

6. Andrew is a sled dog bred by the racing kennel of Alpine Outfitters. He is an Alaskan husky hound cross. In Andrew's case the hound element is saluki, a tall, slender, extremely fast and agile breed. Andrew weighs 60 pounds - large for a racing sled dog. Andrew pulls trainer Steve Capon at an easy run. Notice that his elbows are well below his chest. He can extend his front leg farther forward (for a more efficient gait) than most dogs. Andrew's tug line is extra long to give sufficient distance for safe braking. The 26 inch wheels are bigger than those on most scooters. They are appropriate for rough ground and fast dogs. Steve's wife, Megan Capon, took this photo while riding her cart pulled by three german short hair pointers.

mail, October, 2004: "My first exposure to scooters was in Australia ten years ago, where I saw and heard they had been doing it for some time already, though I don't know exactly how long. We had the first world championship in canicross, bikejoring, scooter one and two dog classes in 2002 in Ravenna, Italy, then last year in Aranda, Spain."

Sled dog sports are growing rapidly. Tim White served as president of the International Federation of Sleddog Sports (IFSS) in 1998. In 2004 the Federation has 38 member federations representing thousands of mushers around the world.

The three main styles of sled dog sports are Nome, Nordic, and Dry land. The Nome style of the sport is performed in snow with a dog sled. Nome style is the most traditional form of dog powered sports, especially in North America. Its name comes from Nome, Alaska.

Nordic sports include skijoring and pulka. In skijoring, the skier skies behind the dog attached by a tug line snapped to a belt around the hips. The skier's arms are free to do the poling. Pulka is like skijoring except that between the skier and the dog is a pulk, a traditional Scandinavian toboggan. The pulk carries supplies that the skier might need for a journey of several days. In a race the pulk carries a specific weight.

7. A bikejorer races in Hungary with his german shorthair pointer. Notice that the dog's tugline is attached to the bicyclist instead of the bicycle. Photo courtesy of Filip Chludil of Czech Republic.

Dry land dog-powered sports are practiced where there is no snow. They use a wheeled vehicle like a scooter. Bikejoring is like scootering except that the human rides a bicycle instead of scooter. Carting is like sledding, but with a three or four-wheeled cart. Carts are used with multiple dogs whereas scooters and bicycles are usually used with one or two dogs.

Dry land mushing without a mechanical device is called canicross - "cani" for dog and "cross" for cross

by Daphne Lewis

8. A European canicross competitor races in the rain with her Irish setter in Hungary. Irish setters are fast, energetic, fun loving dogs. Notice this lovely dog's white face. Old dogs love to run also. Photo courtesy of Filip Chludil.

country. In canicross, the musher runs behind the dog while attached to the dog with a skijor belt. Canicross runners increase their best running speed by a couple miles an hour with the help of their dog.

Dog scootering started late in the United States, well behind Australia, New Zealand and European countries. It has developed slowly. Nome style mushing has dominated. My own dog scooter story began in 1995 when my four-year-old rottweiler and I moved from rural Redmond to urban Seattle, Washington. Now that I lived in the city, I needed to exercise Rubro. I bought a pair of roller blades and we proceeded to skate around an urban lake called Green Lake. Roller blades were limiting: pavement only, daytime only, level ground only and there better not be acorns or twigs on the pavement. And besides Rubro trotted slowly and my feet went to sleep rolling along behind him. I had to think of something he could pull with air filled wheels and brakes. "Aha, a scooter!" In 1996, being on a limited budget, I often drove past the local thrift store hoping that there would be a scooter outside. One day there was. It was a cute scooter with 12-inch wheels. It was sized for children. I bought it for 99 cents and took it to a bicycle store for repair. Repair cost ninety nine dollars. Rubro and I spent many happy weekends exploring mountain bike trails in the hills near Seattle. We clambered over logs, slogged up hills, shoved the little scooter under fallen trees, dodged mud puddles and all in all had a lot of fun. I became hooked on dog scootering. At that time I had a little MacIntosh computer with a black and white screen. From time to time for a year or two, I typed "scooter" into various search engines. I never found a better scooter than my $99.99 cent scooter from the thrift store.

I decided that if I liked dog scootering, other people would also. I wondered if the sport should be called dog scooter or scooter dog. In 1997 I wrote the first edition of "My Dog Likes to Run. I Like to Ride". I spent a couple of months typing after work at night. I was in the flush of excitement. Tim White bought a copy. Tim told me that dog scootering was an established sport in Australia, New Zealand, and Australia. He said that they scooter because there is little snow and because with limited water for individual wells, people live in cities. In cities they can only keep one or two dogs. I was amazed. "So I am not the only person scootering!"

Tim White wrote to me that he believed that children who run their dogs with scooters are more likely to become mushers later in life. When he was race marshall in Poland, he went into Toys R Us and bought scooters to give to children. He encouraged me to promote the sport of dog scootering.

Rubro tore his cruciate ligament a week after "My Dog Likes to Run" arrived from the printer in November of 1997. The other knee tore six months later and the first knee needed a second operation six months after that. Rubro did not scooter for the year following the printing of the book. When he began scootering again, he never moved quickly. He would trot at six miles an hour or walk. I mourned the loss of my demonstration dog just as I was ready to market the book and start a new sport in the U.S. of A.

In 2000, I started the dog scooter talk group **DogsLovetoRun@yahoogroups.com**. I imported ten scooters from Australia and created the DogScooter.com web site. I organized Fun Runs and showed up at a dry land event of the Northwest Sled Dog Club. Ruby and I "ran" (well, "trotted" at six miles an hour) a novice race and enjoyed it thoroughly. It was the first time there had been a rottweiler at the races and I had the only scooter there.

In 2004 Dog Sled Clubs in Michigan, Washington, and New England include scooter races in their Dry land events. Mushers are aware of scooters and are beginning to use them in their training program. Important teachers of mushers like Jamie Nelson and Ann Stead teach mushing clinics called Mushing Boot Camp. Their students

9. Melissa Miller, 13 years old, enjoys a scooter race in Michigan. Melissa wears a bicycle helmet as required in scooter races. Melissa's mother, Jill Miller, organized the race. Photo courtesy of Jill Miller.

are drivers of multiple dog teams. In addition Nelson and Stead teach pull training work shops geared to the owner of a single dog. In these workshops, they use scooters. The Cascade Sleddog Club of Oregon has taught pull classes for scooters since 2001. In 2001 they depended on me to bring a van load of scooters for students to try out. In 2005 the mushers had their own scooters. These scooters lined the fence like a parking lot for scooters.

What Breed of Dog?

You live with your dog seven days a week. You scooter with him for a few hours every week. The best breed for scootering is the one that you love during the many hours that you are not scootering. In other words the breed that you already live with and love is the proper breed to scooter with.

Scooters are EASY to pull. They have wheels! Pull a human friend on a scooter along the sidewalk and see how easy it is. Less force is exerted by a dog pulling a scooter on a sidewalk than the same dog pulling your arm off while walking on a leash. If your dog loves to run and has lots of energy, he is a natural scooter dog.

Dog size is not important - unless you plan to win at races. Some dogs pull hard, some don't pull much at all, regardless of size. At one extreme you are taking the dog for a walk with a scooter instead of a leash. The dog runs in front of you and the tug line is tight but he is tiny and you do most of the propulsion. It is still worthwhile because running is good exercise for the dog and kicking is good exercise for you.

At the other extreme you have medium to large size dogs that are pulling the scooter as fast and as hard as they can go. If these dogs are running at 20 miles an hour, run just one in front of you, rather than two - and always wear a helmet.

Let's say your sheltie drives you crazy with hyper activity. Harness that beautiful little energy machine to a scooter and let her run like crazy around the block. Build up her stamina so she can run several

10. Jessie and Jasmine are miniature poodles. The two sisters are 12 and 13 years old in this photo. Jasmine likes to chase Jessie. Jane Burkey, their owner, hitches Jessie a body length ahead of Jasmine to get Jasmine to chase Jessie and Jessie to work hard to stay in front. The strategy works! Jane rides a scooter with unusually large wheels. Large wheels are easier to pull than small ones.

miles. Alternate between a steady working trot and several minutes of flat-out joyous running. Sure, a larger dog has longer legs and can go more miles in the same amount of time. Practically speaking, people who scooter with a family dog don't measure distance. They measure time. If your sheltie can scooter for half an hour every day and a couple of hours on weekends, isn't that the same as any family dog? The sheltie will travel less far in half an hour than a pointer but he will travel a lot farther than the two of you walking with a leash.

You will enjoy your time scootering with your eager small dog as much as the owner of the longer legged dog. What you love about your athlete is his attitude: his heart and his desire to work. My little short legged pit bull hunkered her body to the ground and ran with joy. I loved scootering with her. Was she actually going fast? Well no, the Italian spinone traveling next to us was just trotting along.

Most dogs, big or small, can pull you easily on level sidewalks. Any dog can pull you when going downhill, obviously. Going uphill, the dog pulls the scooter while you balance it and run or walk beside it - even a large dog, even a husky, can't pull you up a hill. On rough ground you help the dog by scooting. And so by the nature of the way you scooter on flats, downhills and uphills, the size of the dog is less important than his joy in running.

Scootering can exercise both your dog *and* you. The more I kicked with my pit bull, the faster she ran. The faster she ran, the more fun and exercise it was for both of us. In the old days when I scootered with my rottweiler, I was sweaty after a short time in the mountains. I had to kick on rough ground to help move the scooter. I carried the scooter over fallen branches, shoved it under toppled tree trunks, squeezed the brakes going downhill, and walked or jogged beside the scooter going uphill. Yes, dog scootering is exercise for both of you!

If you already own a dog, scooter with that dog whether sheltie or collie, basenji or mastiff. If you are looking for a dog in order to take up the sport of dog scootering, consider what your goals are, where you will scooter and what size car you drive. In general, a long legged, moderate sized dog makes a good scooter dog. If winning races is your goal, consider getting an alaskan husky, eurohound or long legged hunting dog like a pointer. The shelters are full of dogs surrendered by owners because they are too energetic.

If you plan to run two dogs together, it makes sense to choose dogs with similar leg length because length of leg tends to determine gait more than body weight. Dogs with the same length leg can vary in weight as much as 30 pounds. Of course mushers who race match their team much more closely than just matching leg length. On the other hand, some people run dogs whose gaits do not match at all. One dog lopes along while the other dog trots.

by Daphne Lewis

Characteristics of a good scooter dog

Personality

The most important characteristic of the scooter dog is his personality. A scooter dog runs in front of you. He meets oncoming people, dogs, and horses before you do. He needs to be confident that these oncoming people and animals are friendly and non-threatening. You need to be confident that he will not growl, posture, or bite. Once he is trained, he will know to ignore these "distractions" and to go "on by" them.

11. Rubro, the author's rottweiler, ten years old in this photo, pulls seven year old Wyatt Reehill on his scooter/tricycle. Rubro wears an urban trails harness and a two dog tug line. Wyatt wears a helmet. Photo by author.

Scooter dogs often run with other dogs in Fun Runs or races. Their attitude towards these dogs must be calm and accepting. Posturing and dominance are not appropriate. Once at a Fun Run my friend, Cheryl Reehill, put her pit bull, Rage, on a down-stay and went into the rest room. My rottweiler sat down on Rage when I was not looking. When Cheryl came out, Rage gave her a look that said, "I know you like to proof me with distractions, but don't you think having Rubro sit on me is a bit much?" Rage did not growl, snap, fight, stand up or run away. Rage has a perfect temperament for dog scootering - and her down stay is flawless.

Scooter dogs travel on sidewalks, single track trails, and logging roads. Often they wait while you run into the store, stop to look at a view, or visit a bathroom. Should someone come over to pet them, their attitude should be friendly and welcoming. No growling and biting. No "guarding" the scooter.

If you are unsure of your dog's reliability, train him to accept a muzzle. If a greyhound can race at 45 miles an hour with a muzzle, your pooch can scooter with a muzzle. Scootering with a muzzle is better than staying at home in the yard.

12. A Fun Run on a rail trail in western Washington State has five pit bulls pulling and one terrier mix running free. Photo by author.

Attitude

The scooter dog must love to run. People tell me that their husky woo woos when they bring out the harness, that their cattle dog screams with excitement when she sees the scooter, and that their shepherd mix will go get the harness to make scooter time appear. I have heard comments like, "Drake just always seems curious about what might be ahead around the bend. He just keeps running and looking ahead." Drake was a rescue pitbull running in Virginia.

Physique

Physique matters, of course. If two dogs are in equally good physical condition, the one with the better build will run further and faster than the other. The best build depends on what kind of scootering you want to do. Do you want to scooter at a flat out 20 or more miles an hour or do you want a crisp trot at 10 to 12 miles an hour or will a city sidewalk friendly 6 to 10 mile an hour be just fine?

Generally speaking, long legs are more efficient than short ones. Straight front legs are better than bowed ones. A very wide chest is less efficient than a moderate one. Compare the wide chest of the unathletic English bulldog with the narrow chest of the extremely athletic saluki or greyhound.

An efficient gait with front legs stretching far forward (reach) and back legs extending far back (drive) is better than a short choppy one. Shoulder blades that angle allow more reach than shoulder blades that are vertical. Breed standards often say "Shoulder blades well laid back" in order to describe a dog with good reach.

Front legs that form an arch of muscle as they meet in front of the chest are characteristic of dogs that run fast. If the chest from the front looks like a straight horizontal line like my rottweiler, the dog is not a fast running dog. The wide chest gets in the way of the elbow and makes the front end of the dog heavy.

Also characteristic of a fast running dog is an elbow well below the chest. Elbows even with the chest are faster than elbows above the chest.

Slender dogs dissipate heat better than stocky ones. Light coats reflect sun and, therefore heat, better than dark ones. Long muzzles cool more efficiently than short ones. Short muzzled dogs tolerate temperature extremes less well than long muzzled ones and generally have less endurance.

Straight tails indicate a good, strong spine. Tails that curl up over the back are not the best for a fast running endurance dog.

Deaf dogs can scooter. People who run deaf dogs find that the deaf dog has less stress if he is running behind the hearing dog. That way it is easy for him to follow the lead of the hearing dog without having to turn his head sideways. If the dogs are running side by side, the deaf dog's tug line can be a head length shorter than the hearing dogs. Some deaf dogs wear a vibrating collar. When the collar vibrates, the deaf dog turns his head for visual signals.

13. Rogan, a german shorthair pointer, is built to run. His elbows are below his chest. His upper arms form an arch at the point of his chest. His legs are long; he has no extra weight. Rogan is balancing a treat on his nose while posing for this photo. He comes from a line of hunting, not show, pointers. Photo by author.

Equipment

You need a dog, a scooter, a harness, and a tug line.

Harness

Dog scooter harnesses and gear are sold by sled dog outfitters, not by pet stores. Buy the harness locally, if you can, because outfitters have years of mushing experience and gladly answer your questions. It is good to know a local expert.

All scooter harnesses have the basic siwash style. The siwash harness does not bind the shoulders and does not choke the dog. The harness has a fitted collar and a chest strap that goes between the dog's front legs. The design of the harness allows the weight of the scooter to be pulled by the dog's chest, not by his neck and not by his shoulders. The collar does not restrict his breathing because it rests at the intersection of neck and body, not on the neck itself. The harness does not touch or bind the shoulders. Shoulders and front legs move freely. Siwash harnesses are available in traditional and recent styles.

There is no "best harness". Some harnesses fit one body type, and others, another. When you order from a harness maker, you may want to discuss with them which harness will best fit your particular dog. A greyhound may need a different style of harness than a pit bull and a pit bull may need a different harness than a siberian husky.

Traditional Siwash Harness

The traditional siwash is the prototypical sled dog harness. It has the siwash collar and chest strap. A side strap runs from the chest strap, behind the dog's elbows, and along the dog's side to the top of his back where it ends at the base of his tail and joins the strap from the other side. The tug line snaps to the joined side straps at the base of the tail.

The "recreational harness" is the most basic siwash harness. It has collar, chest strap, side straps and loop. It is used for puppies and for wider dogs like Newfoundlands.

by Daphne Lewis

14. An alaskan husky Xpointer and a german short hair pointer model x-back harnesses at a lunch break on a fun run in eastern Washington. They stand in front of their sand lynx cart. Photo by author.

The "x back harness" is the style of siwash harness used most frequently. It is the traditional siwash with the addition of straps that cross the back and form an x. These straps hold the side straps in place. The x back harness fits narrow chested dogs like huskies.

The "h back harness" has two straps that run along either side of the dog's back. This harness fits long backed dogs like german shepherds. It was designed for long distance dogs pulling a load. Some people prefer it to the x back for distance racing because it puts somewhat less pressure on the hips.

Modern Siwash Harness

Jeff King is a three time winner of the Iditarod. He is known for his innovative approach to mushing products and techniques. In 2002 he noted that sled dogs in long distance races develop a sore spot on top of their hips. The sore spot was from the downward pressure of the traditional harness where it ends at the base of the tail. King designed a harness which is similar to a walking or tracking harness and ran with it in the 2003 Iditarod. His dogs performed better than with their former harnesses.

Guard or Manmat harness. Instead of straps continuing up to the base of the dog's tail, the Jeff King design has an adjustable girth encircling the dog's ribs. The tug line attaches to a loop at the top of the girth. There is no pressure on the hips because the loop is near the dog's withers rather than his tail.

Urban Trails Harness. In 2003 Becky Loveless of Alpine Outfitters designed and developed the urban trails harness for scooter dogs. Like the Jeff King harnesses, the back and hips of the dog are free of pressure. The urban trails harness has an adjustable girth and a D ring on top of the girth where the tug line snaps. The urban trails harness works well when the pull angle is upwards. On an average size dog, the tug line slopes upwards from the D ring to the scooter.

When using harnesses that depend on a girth, cinch the girth tightly. The girth must be snug so that the collar is held in place when the dog pulls. If the girth is loose, the harness rocks backwards and the lower part of the collar rides up onto the dog's neck.

Hybrid Performance Harness (Y-back). In 2004 Becky Loveless developed the hybrid performance harness. People who have raced their dogs with traditional harnesses and then tried the hybrid performance harness say that their dogs flex their backs more naturally because there is no pressure on their hips. They run as if they were free running. Choose this harness for scootering if the tug line runs straight back to the scooter. This occurs either because the dog is tall or the attachment point on the scooter is low.

15. Rubro, retired at age eleven, models his urban trails harness. Photo by author.

If you are running a short dog and a long dog side by side, consider putting the urban trails harness on the long dog and the performance hybrid harness on the short dog. This way they can run nose beside nose instead of one ahead of the other.

Harnesses smell bad after a while. Wash them in a washing machine as needed. Hang to dry. Always wash a harness before you send it back to the outfitter for repair or resizing.

16. The pit bull wears a hybrid performance harness. The rottweiler wears an urban trails harness. Neither dog has a neckline so the reluctant old rottweiler runs to the side and behind the eager young pit bull. Photo by Tatsuki Kobayashi.

Measuring

Outfitter web sites describe how to measure your dog. For the urban trails harness and the hybrid performance harness, you need three measurements: collar, breast strap and girth. The top of the harness collar rests at the juncture of the neck and the back which is the forward point of the withers. The bottom of the collar rests at the top of the breast bone. It is important that the collar is big enough that it rides on body muscle and not on the windpipe. With heavily haired dogs, pull the tape measure tight to get an accurate measurement. The girth measurement is taken midway on the ribs well

by Daphne Lewis

behind the dog's elbows and shoulder blades where the ribs split away from the sternum. The girth is adjustable. The length of the breast strap is from the top of the breast bone to the girth.

Outfitters suggest that you measure three times and take an average. Generally they want also the breed of dog and the weight. Some harnesses are sold with the dog's name embroidered on it. Reflective tape for running in the dark costs a few dollars extra.

Tug line

The tug line connects the harness to the scooter. The length of the tug line varies from six to nine feet. Slow dogs trotting on city sidewalks use short lines. You need the dog close to you because buildings obstruct your view around the corner. Fast dogs running on logging roads use long lines. You need distance between you and the dog when going fast.

Skijorers use lines as long as twelve feet. They need the length to keep their skis from touching the dog. Twelve feet gives them room to turn and time to stop. Twelve feet is the maximum length allowed by ISDRA (International Sled Dog Racing Association and IFSS (International Federation of Sleddog Sports).

Most scooterers believe that elasticity in the line makes scootering more comfortable for the dog and the human. Purchased tug lines have the elastic built into them. You can wrap a bungee around the stem of the scooter and attach a strong leash to it to get the same effect.

17. The strap section of the tug line wraps twice around the stem of scooter. The snap clips into the D ring. The tug line thickens where an elastic cord is inserted inside. Photo by author.

I use a tug line designed for dog scootering. Alpine Outfitters of Marysville, Washington, makes it of black polyethylene rope. A bungee is built into the middle section. A brass slide snap is at the dog end and strapping made into an adjustable loop is at the scooter end. Brass is less brittle at lower temperatures than other metals and is preferred by mushers. You can shorten or lengthen the tug line by adjusting the diameter of the loop. To attach the tug line to the scooter, wrap the loop once or twice around the stem of the scooter and snap the snap into the D ring.

There is no need for special attachment hardware on the scooter.

There are single dog tug lines and two dog tug lines. Two dog tug lines can be used for one dog by snapping both snaps to his harness. Two dog tug lines come with a neckline. The neckline is a short line with a snap at both end. The neckline attaches to the collar of each dog. A neckline forces the dogs to run close to each other. Necklines are required in races. Necklines are useful in crowded situations or when head on passing is expected. Necklines are also useful when running a deaf dog or a blind dog. With a blind dog, of course, the guide dog must be steady, gentle, slow, and well trained and the trail should be smooth.

Untrained dogs twist around and tangle their necklines with the tug lines. Necklines are a nuisance with untrained dogs. Train dogs individually to line out before hitching two together. The first few times out, don't use necklines. Should the dogs twist about while waiting to go or stopping along the trail, hold the tug lines up above their backs to prevent tangles.

Necklines can be bought in various lengths and strengths. Strong necklines are useful for lengthening tug lines. Sometimes a long bodied dog is run next to a short bodied one. To have the two run head by head, attach a neckline to the tug line of the shorter bodied dog. Breakable necklines can be special ordered. Weak necklines are a safety feature because they break on impact such as when dogs go around opposite sides of a post. Some people order elastic necklines to give dogs a bit of freedom to pick their route on a trail.

18. Two border collies run single file. The wheel dog is deaf. A deaf dog takes his cues from the other dogs because he can not hear the musher. Running in wheel is easier than alongside the leader because he can follow with less attention. He has time to look around and enjoy the scenery. The wheel dog wears an x back harness. The gang line is designed for two dogs. Its two tugs are attached to the one dog. Photo by CJ Schuler.

To scooter with three dogs, you can run them three abreast in a fan hitch or you can run two as a pair with the third running behind or in front of the paired dogs. On narrow trails, run single file, one dog behind the other. To scooter with four dogs, run one pair in front of another. Most scooterers do not run four dogs because four dogs have too much power for a scooter to control. Of course with small dogs, running four dogs is practical and fun. If you had a houseful of small active dogs

by Daphne Lewis

such as cocker spaniels, jack russell terriers, or miniature schnauzers, you could hitch up four of these dynamos and easily keep up with larger dogs hitched singly.

Scooter

Scooters for dog scootering must have air filled tires and decent brakes. Razor scooters are dangerous. The vertical angle of the stem causes instability at dog speed. The scooters fall apart under the stress of a galloping dog. Many do not have brakes. Their small hard wheels catch in cracks and sink in lawns and gravel.

19. Nicole Royer breaks the rules. She runs four dogs on a scooter! Her team includes a Korean jindo dog (left) and a siberian husky (right) in lead and two alaskan malamutes in wheel. The right side malamute is 8 months old in this photo. Now that he is grown, he is too powerful to run in a four dog team on a scooter. Nicole states that his early scooter trainng helped him become the great working dog he now is: Wencinja's Kodiak Kwest. CD CGC WTD WLD WPD WWPD WWPDX The husky at age 12 still out runs the malamutes. Nicole says that her active life is what has kept the husky so young. Nicole's Rhino scooter has wide tires. "For flatter ground (particularly sand, mud, or snow) and for around the neighborhood you just can't beat this scooter. At 20 or so pounds, it's light weight and it's built to last." Photo and quote courtesy of Nichole Royer.

Some people run their dogs with bicycles instead of scooters. Mountain bikers often choose to ride the bike they already own rather than to purchase a scooter. The choice between bicycle and scooter depends on factors such as breed and keenness to run of the dog, safety of the human, and cost of repairs. First, the dog. My dog, a rottweiler, never trotted faster than 6 miles an hour: too slow to ride a bicycle but fast enough to ride a scooter. Second, safety. When standing on a scooter, your feet are four to six inches from the ground. You are safer than when riding a bicycle. Your feet are free of pedals, your legs are free of cross bars, and your bottom is not resting on a seat. Third, it depends on the cost of repair. A bicycle is more easily damaged than a scooter. When the dog lunges after a deer, tumbling you onto your elbows and dragging the empty scooter at full chase speed, the scooter gets scratched up. Maybe a brake cable detaches. When the dog drags a bicycle, expensive damage to the bicycle can occur. The derailleur, the pedals and the gear shifter may be bent and damaged.

Scooters can be bought from bike stores, dog outfitters, eBay and DogScooter. I bought my first scooter from a thrift store. Some people weld their scooters from BMX bicycles. If you scoot at a trot and weigh less than 140 pounds, a scooter with a 12 inch wheel can suffice while you save for a better scooter with larger wheels. The thrift store scooter that Rubro and I used the first few years was a child's scooter with 12 inch wheels. We used it on pavement in the city and on dirt trails in the mountains. It was easy to fit into a car, lift over logs, squeeze under fallen trees and wait at traffic lights without blocking pedestrians. It is not the scooter I would choose now, but I loved it back then.

The micro scooter by Blauwerk is designed for adults even though it has 12 inch wheels. It is good for slow dependable dogs like my rottweiler. It folds in half so is easy to store in a car for quick spontaneous exercise of you or the dog. If you attend a dog event, you can scooter from your car to your booth and from your booth to the restroom much quicker than walking. Rubro and I frequently left our scooter booth at dog shows and toured the other booths on our way to the restrooms. I laid the scooter on its side and Rubro waited beside it.

The larger the wheel, the easier it is for a dog to pull. Dog scooters usually have wheels sized between 16 and 26 inches. Large people whose dogs cruise along at 18 to 20 miles an hour and sprint at 25 miles per hour will choose 26 inch wheels. The Blauwerk downhill scooter has 26 inch wheels, suspension forks and a high foot platform. See illustration 6.

Most 16 inch scooters are designed for children. They are cheaper and smaller than most 20 inch wheel scooters. In many cases they are the best scooter for getting into the sport. They fit women five feet four inches and less. To adapt them to taller adults, order them with a stem riser to raise the existing handlebar or order a larger handlebar. The larger handlebar requires a longer brake cable. If your dogs train at 15 to 25 miles per hour, do not consider the 16 inch wheel scooters. You need the stability of the larger scooters.

People tend to prefer the scooter they are used to. For example, one of my friends has the mountain scooter by Diggler. It has 20 inch wheels, a snazzy aluminum frame, and quality front shocks. She wouldn't think of using a different scooter. My preference is for the nimble, cheap Torker with 16 inch wheels and a stem riser. I can't be bothered with the large size of the Diggler and she can't be bothered with my toy. I have a slow dog and she has fast ones.

Large diameter tires are easier to pull over rough ground than small ones. Street tires are easier to pull than knobby tires. Well inflated tires roll more easily than under-inflated ones. Expensive scooters roll more easily than cheap ones because they have better bearings and hubs. If you are running with a small fast dog like a whippet, you might decide to buy a scooter that is very easy to pull with 20 inch wheels, top of the line hubs, and street tires. On the other hand if you have two Presa canarios each weighing 120 pounds, you have plenty of power. Your concern is to stop the team if they are determined to chase a deer through the woods. You can stop them if you are riding the brawny mountain diggler with knobby tires and mountain bike brakes. You could not stop them on my small Torker scooter.

Some scooters have shock absorbers. For high speed dogs on rough ground, shock absorbers are essential. Without them, you are out of control and terrified. For trotting dogs on city sidewalks and jogging trails, shock absorbers are unnecessary. Your bent knees are sufficient. Forks with shock absorbers are heavier than those without.

Large diameter tires have more rotational mass than smaller tires. At speed on tight turns they are harder to turn. In a race with numerous twists and turns, you may find 20 inch wheels easier to handle than 26 inch wheels. A scooter that is new to the U.S. is the diggler scooter with a 20-inch wheel in front and a 16-inch wheel in back. This scooter will ride the straight aways at speed and yet handle switch backs with aplomb. It will fit into mini-vans more easily than the scooter with two 20-inch wheels.

Fenders keep your clothes clean and the rocks out of your eyes. Without fenders the rear tire flings mud up your back and the front tire throws it up your front. I have seen my friends with brown stripes up to their necks. On dry trails the knobby tires may from time to time sling a pebble at your face. Fenders make sense. Twenty inch tires throw more mud and higher than sixteen inch ones.

Scooters get flat tires from thorns and broken glass. Ask your bicycle shop what they recommend to reduce flats. Mechanics have strong preferences and what is best changes from year to year. More resistant inner tubes can be bought for a little extra cost.

Narrow platforms are best if you are scooting without the dog because kicking is easier. Your kicking leg stays closer to you. The edge of a narrow foot platform lines up with the tubes that support it. When you pick up the front of the scooter to lift it over a curb or log, the back end tends to fall into your leg. The width of tube plus platform reduces the discomfort of the blow.

Most people prefer the wide long foot platforms provided by the Diggler scooters. You can move your feet around on the scooter depending on the speed and terrain. And these platforms are built like skateboards; they grab the bottoms of your shoes. The drawback is that they extend beyond the supporting tubes. When you lift over a curb, the platform hits your shin with a narrow edge. Some people take to wearing shin guards.

Many scooterers, especially mushers, rarely assist the dog. It is a training principle with them. Other scooterers routinely kick to assist either because the dog is small or because they can go faster if they help the dog. If you assist the dog, do so in such a way that the tension on the tug line remains constant. Scoot rhythmically. Kick three times on one side. Switch feet smoothly and then kick three times on the other. It is easier to kick from a narrow low footboard than a higher wider one.

When choosing a scooter, consider how you will transport it. Scooters are longer than bicycles with the same size wheels because of the length of the foot platform. Scooters with 16-inch wheels easily fit in the back of an SUV. Scooters with 20-inch wheels fit into an SUV if the rear wheel tucks beside the folded middle seat. Bungee the scooter upright to a hand grip on the ceiling to leave space for the dog and gear. Scooters with 20 and 26 inch wheels have quick release hubs.

Many people carry their scooters on bicycle racks. Some rear mounted racks carry the scooters upside down. Diggler foot platforms are made with anti-skid tape glued to the top of the aluminum platform. Pad the bars of the bike rack to prevent the tape scratching off. Run a bicycle lock cable through the spare tire hub and around the scooter to lock the scooter to the car. Secure the handle bars so they do not revolve in the wind. A sixteen inch wheel scooter will ride behind the car on the bike rack. A 20 inch scooter is longer and would stick out to either side of most vehicles. If they must ride on the rack, remove a wheel or two.

Check the tire pressure of the scooter before running the dogs. It is easy to pump them up with a bicycle pump.

Dog

The most interesting equipment for dog scootering is the dog. Presumably you already live with this pleasure seeking, fascinating creature. You may find as you get into the sport of scootering that you look at dogs differently. Your head swirls around when you see a dog who looks like a runner. "Gee, that dog looks fast. I bet he can run like a deer", says that uncontrollable part of the brain that talks to you. And the irresponsible part of your brain answers, "If I got one more dog, I could go faster." The responsible part of your brain is saying, "You already have a dog". And the argument goes on. This brain conversation can drive you crazy. Another crazy making conversation is "He thinks his dog is faster than my dog."

Mushers say, "The first ride is free". They are talking about the addiction that got them to get that second dog, and then the third, and then they took up racing and changed to a faster breed and then... Dog scootering is an inexpensive sport as long as you have just one dog and one scooter. "Maybe I should get one more dog. Two isn't too much. And maybe I need a better scooter..." This expansion into multiple dogs is where scootering becomes expensive. With multiple dogs you need a bigger car and a bigger yard - and more scooters and then a cart and you had best have a great relationship with your vet.

Dog scootering is good for the sport of mushing. Dog scooterers are a pool of talent from which new mushers spring. While most dog scooterers keep their sanity and do

by Daphne Lewis

not become mushers, they do become the fans that eagerly follow mushing races. They go on-line to follow the Iditarod day by day. They know top winning mushers by name and photo. They buy books like "Winning Strategies for Distance Mushers" by Joe Runyan, "My Lead Dog was a Lesbian" by Patrick O'Donoghue, and the fabulous and hilarious "Winter Dance" by Gary Paulsen.

Additional Equipment and Supplies

Besides the dog, harness, tug line and scooter, you will usually take additional supplies.

Water and bowl - Dogs drink lots of water on scooter runs. Your ordinarily water indifferent dog is likely to love water when scootering.

Special treats - It is fun to give special treats that are given only when scootering. Some dogs love scootering so much they hate to turn around and go back to the car. When the dog gets to the car, the best hot dogs in the world or a can of sardines and good clean water should be waiting for him. "Go to the car" should cause a burst of speed at the end of the run.

Poop bags - Don't leave poop on the trail. Whether you pick up the poop or kick it off the trail depends on where you are scooting.

Helmet, wrist guards, etc. - Wear safety gear if you have a fast dog. Experienced scooterers wear helmets, padded coveralls, leather gloves and leather boots. They also wear *goggles*. Knobby tires throw pebbles in your face. The paws of galloping dogs throw sand. When scooterers fall, they tend to fall on their elbows because their hands are gripping the brake levers. They break their elbows. Elbow pads make sense with fast dogs, especially when traveling on pavement.

> Amy Christenson, recreational and sprint musher in Colorado, writes an e-mail to the DogsLovetoRun@yahoogroups.com in fall, 2004.
>
> *My main leader kept the speed down in that area the next time through. I think she knows my limitations better than I do!*
>
> *I've had the same helmet for like 6 years or so and I always wear it because I "should" (and it keeps my head warm). I've had my share of spills including one lovely broken collar bone but never have actually hit my head - until today. Running my two fastest adults in crappie weather (read by dogs as incredibly fun). So much fog I could maybe see 5 feet in front of them and semisolid "muck" making the single-track trail hard to read and unforgiving. I had successfully navigated many rut/mud spots and was almost back to the truck when I zigged and should have zagged and ended up plowing headfirst into a bush. My head literally stopped us. The dogs waited patiently for me to right myself and I was very happy that I had no pain or injury. Love that helmet! Dirty but still intact.*

Boots - You need boots or at the very least hiking shoes to scoot safely. You may need to jump off the scooter unexpectedly or to lift the scooter over a log while the dog continues running. You may need to slam on the brakes and drag your foot for additional stopping power. Do not wear sandals!

Lights, reflectors - In winter, you scooter in the dark. Buy head lamps from sporting goods stores or army surplus stores. Some harnesses and scooters come with reflectors on them. Add these items if they do not come with your equipment. Wear a reflective pinnie over your coat. DogScooter sells pinnies designed for dog scootering. Pet stores sell blinking lights to attach to collars and harnesses.

Other items - Carry extra items such as a fold up raincoat, first aid kit, and a map. Carry them in a fanny pack or handlebar bag. Many people carry bicycle tools for tightening handlebars and repairing flat tires.

Booties - Booties protect dog feet from hot pavement, sharp gravel, and ice crystals. Some dogs run better with booties when the ground is uncomfortable. It is a good idea to carry some booties with you in case of a foot injury. Most scooterers do not need booties because they don't run the mileage or the speed that mushers do.

Speedometer - Got to have a speedometer! Speedometers tell you your current speed and, when the trip is over, they tell you miles traveled, maximum speed, average speed, and elapsed time. How can you brag if you don't really know how fast Lightning ran? Or how far Long Legs ran last night? As your dog's coach, a speedometer is your ticket to performance.

GPS - Some scooterers use gps units to assist in their training. With it they can accurately log their training miles. It is easy to overestimate mileage.

Training Log - Some people keep a training log on paper; others, on computer. The information contained in the training log varies with what you want to know.

Dog Health & Safety

You are your dog's coach. You trained him to scooter; now you must condition him for running. And you are responsible for his health and safety. The same issues that concern you as a pet dog owner (veterinary care, healthy food, safe enclosures, etc.) concern you as a scooter dog coach. In addition there are safety issues specifically related to scootering: These include foot and nail care, weight management, hydration, heat stress, and muscular/skeletal care.

Foot and nail - Pads can wear from running on pavement. Scooterers prefer to run their dogs on dirt. When running on pavement they slow the dogs to a trot. Speed is reserved for softer surfaces. Some scooterers put booties on their dogs when running on crushed rock and pavement. It depends on the dog. Some have tough pads and some do not. Some scream and holler to go and dig into the pavement. These dogs are susceptible to tearing their pads.

Nails are an extension of the toe bone. If they are too long, they change the alignment of the toes when the foot lands and pushes off. Dogs get traction from their pads, not from their nails. Long nails interfere with traction. Mushers say that a toenail is the proper length if the nail is an eighth of an inch above ground when the dog is standing with his weight on his foot. Another measure of proper length is that the toenails are quiet when the dog walks across a floor. Nails are too long if they click on the floor. For a healthy scootering foot, trim those nails. Mushers trim two weeks before a race to be sure healing has occurred should they cut too close.

Weight Management - Pet dogs only eat what we give them. They can't open the fridge and help themselves. They can't leave the yard and raid neighbors' garbage cans. It should be easy to keep them slim and trim.

Megan Capon shares her knowledge about foot care.

My dogs will 'slip' their pads under the right circumstances, especially Rogan who has an overabundance of enthusiasm and not a shred of self-preservation instinct. Genetics, gait, and size play a role in foot wear... my whispy #35 pound german shorthair pointer girls have hardly any problems, and Andrew, the giant alaskan husky, we borrowed last season never had foot problems either.

Pads CAN get toughened up over time, but that means you have to carefully monitor wear on them through the process and apply boots BEFORE the pads are damaged. The pads will get slicker and thinner, and when they're really worn, I'll often see little 'pinpricks' of moisture. This is a sign to BOOT NOW, because after this you'll be getting into pink and a limping dog. Terrain and distance obviously makes a difference in foot wear. I start dogs on dirt in the fall, let their feet toughen up on short runs and/or boot when needed... later on they'll be able to take on more gravel and finally some (unavoidable) pavement. I still notice a difference in how individual dogs wear, Princess Dulcie's feet and nails being made out of something like, oh, hardened steel- LOL! JMO: boots are cheap from any mushing supplier, so might as well try several kinds out. Just be sure to have any ol' boots ready when you need them! Fleece tend to hold heat in but supply some padding; some cordura wears better than others, etc. I was taught by several highly experienced mentors to apply boots AS TIGHT AS POSSIBLE just before takeoff, then to loosen the velcro up or take them off when stopped for more than a minute or immediately when done running. Not everyone agrees with this, but mine sure don't stay on any other way.

(continued on next page)

Apparently it is not. A large percentage of U.S. dogs is overweight. Many are obese. Obviously it is not safe for a fat dog to scooter. He would tire and overheat easily and could damage joints.

Looking down at a fat dog; you see that the dog is shaped like a sausage. He has no waistline. Look down on the back of a dog at the proper weight and you can see an indentation between his rib cage and pelvis. The dog has a waistline. Run your hand down the spine of a fit dog and you can feel the vertebrae and hip bones. Look at the dog from the side and see a nice tuck up between the ribs and the knee. Some breeds have more tuck up than others but in no breed should the belly hang down. Run your hand along his side. You should be able to feel the ribs. Fat feels soft and hides the ribs. On a thin coated dog at proper weight, you can see the ribs. If the ribs stick out, then the dog is too thin.

I give my dogs a raw beef bone on the three days a week that I leave the house for the day. The bones are wonderful entertainment; the dogs love them and they keep their teeth and gums healthy. However, bones are fattening. On bone days I cut back on their food.

> *(continued from last page)*
>
> *When a dog tears its pad, I try to rinse it off (if the dog hasn't cleaned it out pretty well already), boot the dog, and get home. At home I tend to leave such shallow abrasions open and the dog in a dry area. I've never had a problem with them picking at their feet too much, especially if it dries out. If it's more of a slice I close it with medical glue and might put a fleece boot on rather loosely so the dog can get around more comfortably (and so the carpet doesn't get dotted with blood), but that's ONLY if I'm there to monitor it- dogs can chew up and eat boots, causing a much bigger medical disaster! Their kennel is roofed and dry so I take off any boots before leaving them for the day.*
>
> *ZINC MAKES A HUGE DIFFERENCE!!! It takes a while to become effective, but I have had to use MUCH fewer boots and MUCH fewer foot injuries since getting the HowlingDog suppliment (which has worked better for us than any other zinc I've tried FWIW). It's also ridiculously economical even for multiple dogs. As Cheryl mentioned, however, it DOES require more toenail maintenence... I had to buy an industrial strength nail clipper after we started feeding zinc.*
>
> *Conditioning, proactively applied boots, glue when needed, and supplemental zinc have been our steady standbys through thousands of miles.*

20. Millie, the rescue pitbull, is a few pounds too heavy because the ribs closest to her waist are not individually visible. She has a smooth tuckup and a nice waistline so she is far from fat, however.

Hydration - For working sled dogs, hydration is a very important part of health and safety. An hour or two before a race or training run, mushers give water to their dogs. Many huskies are reluctant drinkers so the mushers bait the water with something to make it taste good. They also give water after the run. The dogs are so hot and thirsty that the water does not need to be baited. Often, though, mushers add special powders that speed recovery from muscle exhaustion - a doggy sports drink.

When we first started scootering in Washington State, we carried water with us in fanny packs. We stopped frequently and gave water to dogs at each stop. Now that we have learned to water the dogs an hour or two before the run, the dogs are not thirsty at these stops. We offer the water but the dogs mostly ignore it.

My new routine to get water into my dogs is to feed a cup of kibble in the morning floating in several cups of water. Often I put a whole raw egg into the water also. The dogs drink all the water in order to get the kibble. They eat the egg and its shell. At night they get a raw chicken leg or back or neck. Raw food has a high water content.

If your dog is well hydrated and you are only running for half an hour you may not need to carry water. Anything longer than that, though, carry water and offer it when the tongue gets long. We stop running when tongues get long, offer water, and resume running when tongues shorten up and dogs start playing again.

Heat Stress - Dogs can overheat and collapse when exercising on warm days. As your dog's coach, pay attention to the heat. Use caution when the weather is warm. Most coaches will not scooter (except short trips like to the store) when the temperature is above 70 degrees. Many scooterers switch activities in summer. They swim, do weight pull, or go hiking.

Should your dog overheat, cool him immediately. Get him into the shade. From your water bottle, squirt water down his throat. Squirt water onto his skin through parted hair. Douse his feet into a water bowl; drape his ear leather into the water bowl also. Better yet get him into a pond or stream. Depending on the severity of his collapse you may need to rush him to a vet. Once a dog has overheated, he is more susceptible to overheating in the future.

Southern dogs acclimate to heat that would destroy sled dogs from the north. While mushers in Alaska consider 50 degrees Fahrenheit to be too hot to run their dogs, scooterers in Florida are grateful when the weather cools to 70 degrees. A significant difference is that the musher's dogs run for many miles. The Florida scooterer might be content with trotting and loping 2 to 10 miles. The working sled dogs are running fast at 15 to 20 miles an hour. A scooter dog may be trotting along at a comfortable 6 to 10 mph.

My friend, Cheryl Reehill, stops scootering in summer. This summer she took up weight pulling with her scooter dogs. Her dogs are doing great in the heat and as their fitness increases they are buffing up and able to do more and more work. Come fall these dogs will be in awesome condition for scootering.

A fit dog acclimated to warm weather is far more resistant to overheating than the average dog. A bikejorer in Texas runs his staffordshire bull terriers and boston terrier at 100 degrees. His route includes a stop at cold water pools every 10 minutes. He does not resume running until his little dynamos have cooled down.

Common sense and awareness are key to avoiding overheating. In warm weather scooterers choose trails that run in the shade of trees. They choose routes that go to swimming holes. They hydrate the dogs well and carry water. In Florida dedicated scooterers run at 1 am, the coolest time of the day. Watch the tongue. It gets longer and longer as the dog needs to cool off more. When too hot, the tongue begins to turn blue. Stop, rest, cool and water the dog, <u>before</u> he is that hot! And perhaps abort the trip and walk him back to the car.

Muscular/skeletal - There is a great deal of discussion among dog fanciers about when to start working a puppy. Breeders of large breeds caution about exercising a puppy too much before the growth plates at the ends of the bones complete their growth. What is too much? I believe that the larger problem is what is too little?

My opinion about exercising young dogs rests on analogy. Children play sports like soccer, basketball, and track. They play games like kick-the-can, tag, and roller skating. These physical activities help them grow strong and able. They do not damage growth plates and cause bone problems later in life. To me scootering is like kids being kids and leading an active physical life. The way a pet dog owner scooters with his puppy or young dog, is the way kids play sports. When the puppy is bouncing with energy, you scooter. When he's tired, you stop. I don't see how you can make a puppy run until his growth plates are damaged. Puppies stop when tired.

I take the breeders' warnings to heart, though, with my puppy. Recently I ran her in a fun run with other dogs. She kept up very well and ran fast. I love going fast. After we got back to the car, other scooterers wanted to run a different trail. I decided not to run Tess again in case that would be too much for her. It certainly was nothing for the older dogs. I also did not run her again because I wanted to stop when she was performing enthusiastically and running fast and hard.

I vary Tess' activity a lot. Sometimes she chases a ball or plays tug of war. Sometimes she drags a tire and other times runs free in front of me on a trail looking for rabbits or whatever. Sometimes she scooters and sometimes she pulls a cart. When she is older than a year, I will scooter more consistently to build her stamina.

Mushers' livelihoods depend on breeding and training sound, fast dogs. Their pups start in harness at 6 months. The pups run short distances at slow speeds. When they are a year, the work increases but never as long, fast and grueling as the older dogs. The top sled dogs are still sound at 10 years of age. They can serve as recreational sled dogs several years beyond that. If it is OK for musher's pups, it is OK for scooter dogs also.

Training the Dog to Pull a Scooter

Commands

Gee & Haw - "Turn right" & "Turn left". Gee and haw are traditional commands for draft animals. They are wonderful old words whose derivation is lost in our European animal powered past.

Over gee - Move over to the gee side of the trail and run there. The opposite is "Over haw". Use "over gee" when there is oncoming traffic. In urban situations, the dog should run on the gee side of the sidewalk always, like a bicycle.

Go straight - "Continue straight ahead. Don't take the other possible route(s)."

This way - Sometimes there is no clear path to follow. Say "This way" and aim the scooter. The dog takes his direction from the heading of the scooter.

Come haw - "Turn to your left and come back towards me." (Make a U turn to the left.) The opposite is "Come gee". Some people say "Gee come" and "Haw come". Some skijorers say "Come around". They don't care which way the dog turns.

On by - "Keep going. Go on by the distraction." Sometimes you use this command to pass a loose dog. Sometimes, to pass a customary stopping place. For example if I am going to the post office which is farther than the grocery store, I tell Rubro "On by" when he starts to turn into the grocery store parking lot.

Ready - I say this before the command "Pull".

Pull - People use various commands to start the dog pulling. Some dogs are so hyped to go that all you say is "OK" and release the brakes. I use "Pull" because I use it for drag training with a tire.

Hike - Some scooterers mean "Start pulling"; others mean "Go faster". Still others mean "Run like crazy!" It helps to excitedly say, "Hike! Hike! Hike!"

Easy - "Slow down". Say it slowly and low.

Get up - "Go faster." Some people say "Hike it up!"

Walk - Use "Walk" when you are on a crowded sidewalk or to cool the dog down. At the beginning of a hill, I run beside the scooter while my dog pulls it at a trot. When I run out of breath, I say "Walk". I also say "Walk" when carrying the scooter up or down a flight of stairs. I do not want my dog to pull me over.

This foot - "Pick up the foot I am touching so I can put it into the harness".

Say hello - Move in a friendly manner towards the person who is admiring you. City scooter dogs waiting at traffic lights get lots of "Your dog sure is pretty. May I pet him?"

Stand - Stand is a useful command when adjusting harnesses, and when there are two or more dogs to harness. Once the dog knows "line out", you do not need "Stand".

Stay - Stay here until I return. When going into a store, unsnap the tug line from the harness and attach it to the collar. Unsnap the other end from the scooter and attach it to an immovable object.

Wait or Whoa - "Whoa" said low and drawn out is more typically used than "Wait". I use "wait" because my dogs already know the word and because "whoa" sounds like 'no' and 'go'.

Line out - "Hold the line out straight and tight while facing away from the scooter." With this command you can harness the dog, attach the tug line, walk back to the scooter, pick it up, give the command to pull and the dog will pull in the direction you want him to go.

Go potty - The dog is working when pulling a scooter. He is not free to pee on bushes. Before hooking him to the scooter, walk him around so he can relieve himself.

Go to the car - This command allows you to speed up the last leg of a scooter run. It saves you when you are lost because your dog is not lost. Some mushers say "Take me home."

by Daphne Lewis

Mush - Mushers do not use "mush" as a command. "Mush" derives from French fur trappers saying "Mouche´" meaning "go fast". Some people say it comes from "Marche´."

Manners

Dogs can be a nuisance and even a menace in the community. As anyone who owns dogs and works with them in an organized sport knows, laws are continually proposed that restrict dog owners' ability to keep dogs. To protect our privilege to own dogs, it is imperative that dog scootering people be sensitive to other people and their opinions. Respect other people's fear of and allergies to dogs. For example, if you are scootering on a city sidewalk or in a city park, always give way to pedestrians. Get off the scooter and walk beside it. You might even have the dog heel beside you, depending on the situation. You don't want your slobbery, friendly pooch out in front of you greeting little children and scaring their mothers. At a traffic light, walk the scooter up beside the dog so as not to hog space on the sidewalk.

Skateboarders are prohibited from certain sidewalks and parking lots. We do not want dog scooterers prohibited also. I for one want to be able to scooter to Starbucks any time and sit and drink coffee and read the paper. No gasoline to buy, exercise quotient met, socializing proceeding on schedule.

Pick up poop. Carry two bags per dog with you on every outing.

When I first started scootering, Rubro and I drove to Cougar Mountain, a nature park, on weekends. We picked up a map at the parking lot and tried out different single track trails each visit. It remains my favorite place to scooter. Singles, couples, families walked the trails. Horses trotted on some trails but not the more delicate ones. A sign at the parking lot said, "No bicycles". I figured that my dog scooter lacked the two major drawbacks of bicycles and therefore was allowed. First, mountain bikers go fast. They do not mix well on single track trails with walkers looking at birds and plants. My Rubro never went fast. Second, bikes dig into the trail with their rear wheel and leave nasty ruts. We did not fit the bicycle description because Rubro trots slowly and the scooter is propelled by a dog, not a trail gauging, poop spraying horse. I figured the rule of "No bicycles" did not apply to me.

I decided to organize Fun Runs. At my first Fun Run I was the only person who showed up. At my second Fun Run two people showed up. One rode a unicycle; the other rode a scooter. I held my third fun run at Cougar Mountain. Fifteen scooters showed up. I was almost speechless with surprise.

After the Fun Run, I received a letter from the Parks department requiring that we never come back. We scooterers impacted the quiet purpose of the park with our numbers and speed and trail hogging! Don't lose the privilege of dog scootering. Be considerate of other trail users! Do not make my mistake.

Some trails are for multiple use including horses. Always when you see or hear a horse, pull off the trail, lay the scooter on its side, down your dog and hold his collar. Some horses are used to everything and would not care if you scootered by them. Others are perplexed and frightened by the combination of person, scooter and dog. A frightened horse can buck its rider off or run away out of control. Do not take the chance of frightening a horse.

Training

While we scooterers are proponents of training scooter dogs carefully, some dogs naturally charge ahead pulling the scooter. Hitch these dogs up and go. You are heavier and stronger than a single dog and the scooter has brakes. You will be able to control the dog. With a natural puller and runner, you can train commands while scootering. Your incorrigible pound puppy will become your prized scooter dog. It is best if these dogs know basic commands such as "Wait", "OK", "Leave it", "Stay", "Let's go" and their name.

Dogs being trained for scootering divide into five groups.

- The dog who charges ahead pulling on the leash.
- The dog who walks with loose leash at your side.
- The very young puppy.
- The older puppy, leggy and full of energy.
- The dog who has experienced dogs to learn from.

Order Harness, Tug line, and Scooter.

Dog Outfitters make sled dog harnesses. Outfitters advertise in sled dog magazines like "Mushing", "Sled Dog Sports" and "Team & Trail". They list their web sites on SledDogCentral.com. Their sites describe their harnesses and how to measure the dog for proper fit.

Order your harness and tug line. For pointy chested dogs like pharaoh hounds, look for harnesses with double straps side by side. The double straps form around the point of the chest. For a puppy, order a puppy harness or recreational harness because they are cheaper than more complicated harnesses. For young puppies the design of the harness is not critical. A pet store harness is OK because the puppy pulls token weight for short periods.

Order your scooter from your local bicycle store, DogScooter.com, or some other source that you discover. Some people find a welder who will make their scooter from BMX bicycles; others do their own welding. Check the links page on DogScooter.com for instructions on making a scooter.

Harnesses are for pulling. Collars are for loose leash walking!

Do not use a flexi-lead with a scooter dog. Flexi-leads teach the dog to pull on his collar, sniff and pee whenever and wherever he wants, zig and zag across the sidewalk, and to stop and start erratically.

While waiting for the harness, teach the commands "walk", "hike", "easy", and "whoa". Take the dog for his walk. Tell him "Walk" and walk along. Say "Hike" and speed up to a trot. Continue at a trot. Say "Hike" again and move into a run. Run for a while. Say "Easy" and slow down to a trot. Practice gradual transitions from one speed to another. You want a scooter dog to slow down gradually, not abruptly. If he slows or stops suddenly while pulling his scooter, you will crash into him.

When your dog understands Hike, Easy, Walk, and Whoa, start teaching turns. As you walk along, exaggerate your turns. Say "gee" just before turning right and "haw" before turning left.

When the harness arrives, put it on the dog. Gather the harness into a circle and put the dog's head through the circle. Then pick up one front leg and bend the paw back at the wrist. Put the bent leg through the arm hole. Do the same for the opposite leg. Smooth out the harness so it rests comfortably at the juncture of neck and torso. The buckle collar rides on the neck above the harness collar. Pull backwards on the tug loop to be sure the harness strapping is flat, comfortable and smooth over the fur.

If your harness is an urban trails or hybrid performance harness, there is one arm hole, not two. After the leg is in the arm hole, buckle the girth. Tighten it so that it will not slip over the skin. It will move as the skin moves on the rib cage. Adjust the location of the chest strap to center on the chest. If the chest strap is off center, it will ride in the dog's arm pit.

Most dogs are indifferent to the harness. Wearing a harness is no big deal. Some dogs are sensitive and need a little conditioning before they are comfortable with harnessing and the harness. With these dogs you can coax them to put their heads through the harness by luring their heads through the collar with a treat. Soon they will offer to put their heads through the harness.

Once you have the harness and tug line, you can teach the dog to walk in front of you whenever the leash is attached to the harness. I have my old dog walk beside me when the leash is attached to the collar. When I attach it to the harness, I say "Up Front" and he walks in front of me. When we come to a hill, I attach the leash to the harness and up the hill he pulls me. We generally jog up hill and walk other places.

You also can teach "Line out". Attach the tug line to something immovable like a fence or sofa. Bring the dog on leash in harness to the unattached end of the tug line and snap it to his harness. Guide him with the leash or a treat until he is holding the tug line tight and is facing away from the immovable object. Tell him "Line out". Move to one side. Guide him back into position should he follow you. Move to the other side. Soon he will get the idea of standing still while holding the line out tight. Drop the leash. Walk around. Guide him with the leash or lure him with a treat should he move. After several practice periods, you will be able to walk behind the dog while he continues to hold the line out straight. Work on this command until he will hold the line out tight regardless of whether you are in front of him or back by the scooter.

For the trained dog, the reward for lining out is running.

1) The dog who charges ahead pulling at the leash

Some dogs are afraid of the scooter. All dogs could become afraid if the scooter fell on them or ran into them. Introduce the dog to the scooter carefully to prevent fear or to alleviate existing fear. The attitude you want to create is "Oh boy! The scooter is great!" Let the dog sniff the scooter and perhaps retrieve treats off it. Do not let the scooter tip over and make a loud noise. Take the dog for a walk on leash while you push the scooter. He should become indifferent to the scooter pretty soon. If your dog continues to be afraid, do whatever it takes to allay the dog's suspicion. You can take the scooter into your house and lay it on its side. Put treats on the scooter. Load the scooter into the car. Do errands with the dog and scooter riding together in the car. Let the dog see you scooting with the scooter.

Some dogs see the scooter's turning wheels as prey. These dogs want to chase and bite at the wheels. With these dogs, line out training is extremely important. Lining out facing away from the scooter is alternate behavior to charging the scooter and biting its wheel. I saw a novice dog suddenly charge the rear tire of a scooter and with one bite puncture the tire. The scooter was not even moving at the time and the dog was on leash ten feet away until he charged pulling the leash from the person's hand.

Confident and exuberant dogs pull on the leash because they want to get somewhere. They want to run. With a dog like this, you can start scootering once he is happy in the harness and happy walking along with you while you push the scooter. You can return to ground training later as you see the need.

by Daphne Lewis

Take the dog, the scooter and a friend to a safe trail. If your dog is accustomed to veering right and left on a particular sidewalk or trail while on a Flexi-lead, take him to a trail that is new to him. Choose a trail that is enclosed by woods, if practical.

Put the harness on the dog. Attach the tug line to the harness and to the scooter. Have the friend walk beside the scooter while you walk beside the dog with a leash to his collar. The dog pulls the scooter; the friend merely keeps it upright behind the dog. The dog may startle when he feels the pull on his harness from the scooter. You can jolly him with words or treats. When he is over the startling, you can jog along. The friend will jog along while holding the scooter upright. Moving quickly is fun for the dog. The friend can hop on the scooter and you can continue running beside him.

It may be wise to stop at this point. Be sure to stop at a successful point. On the other hand, you know your dog. If he is eager to run, you can move to the next step. Hop on your bicycle and entice the dog to chase you while pulling the scooter with your friend riding on it.

Stop before the dog is tired. Say, "go to the car". At the car, offer water and extra tasty treats. Perhaps serve them on the scooter platform.

The next training session, have your friend ride the bicycle while <u>you</u> ride the scooter. Your dog may suddenly realize that you <u>want</u> him to run. He may take off freely down the trail. This will be a thrill for both of you. Stop sooner than your dog wants to stop. You may have to go back to you riding the bike and the friend the scooter, but probably not.

My little pit bull was a headstrong dog who pulled on the leash and always walked in front of me. She loved to pull so much that all I did was to aim her down the trail, hop on the scooter, and enthusiastically cheer, "Go Millie, go, go, go." She got into the spirit of it and started running happily.

Some people train their scooter dogs solely when they ride the scooter. Others go back to ground training. If your dog only pulls when pulling is easy, go back to training with a drag. Make the drag heavy enough for the dog to work a bit to pull it. Drag on the flat and drag up a hill. "Guess what dog? You <u>can</u> pull up hill" and also "Don't stop when it gets hard to pull. Pull harder!"

If you will be running two dogs side by side, teach them about necklines first. Neckline them together and let them run free for five minutes. Do this three days in a row. They will learn to run together.

2) The dog who walks with loose leash at your side.

The initial training is the same for both the always-pulling dog and the loose leash dog. Make sure the dog is at ease with wearing his harness and with the scooter. The dog should not be afraid of the scooter whether on its side, upright, or moving beside or behind him.

Ground Training

Put on the harness. Snap one end of the tug line to the dog's collar and the other end to the harness. Stand beside the dog in heel position. With your right hand, hold the tug line near the collar and with your left hand hold the tug line near the the harness. Tell the dog to walk forward. While you are walking along beside the dog,

21. A siberian husky is learning to pull. One end of a tug line is snapped to his collar and the other to his harness. The end of the tug line that is attached to his collar has little or no weight on it. The end that is attached to the harness is pulled backwards as if a scooter were attached. Photo by author.

pull backwards on the harness with your left hand. This backwards pull mimics the "weight" of the scooter. The weight may confuse the dog. He has been taught not to pull against his collar. Encourage him to walk forward by using your forward command and by quick tugs forward with your right hand on the tug line next to the collar. I use "Pull" for my forward command. Walk along briskly keeping steady backwards pressure on the harness with your left hand. Praise excitedly as the dog keeps up with you while pulling against your left hand.

22. The siberian husky is now walking in front of his owner. The owner is applying pressure to the harness. This is ground training. Commands such as "gee' and "haw" and "easy" and "on by" can be taught with ground training.

Once the dog understands to pull against the harness while walking beside you, you can break into a run. Running may excite the dog enough that you can let go of the tug line with your right hand. Run near his haunches while continuing to pull backwards against the harness with your left hand.

by Daphne Lewis

Ground training includes all work where you walk behind the dog. Work him until he pulls on the word "pull" and continues to pull until you say "Whoa". He should walk in front of you for the full length of the tug line. You can train at a walk. Speed is not necessary. The dog is learning to pull with the harness and to walk in front of you. You can also do this at a run.

Pull training with the double ended tug line is ground training. Ground training is underused. Consider using it whenever a training issue comes up. A typical issue is "How do I keep my dog from stopping to pee all the time?" Hitch him to the double ended leash. Walk down the trail with him pulling in front of you. The second he attempts to move to the side to sniff or pee, tell him, "On by". If he continues down the trail, "Good dog!". If he begins to veer off trail, correct him quickly with the leash to his collar. As soon as he is going well again, "Good dog!" Ground training is excellent for training Gee Over, Haw Over, and On by.

When your dog knows to walk in front of you while pulling a drag and accepts the scooter, you can hitch him to a scooter. Follow the guidelines above for the Dog that Forges Ahead.

Drag Training

Do not hitch your dog to your scooter if he is afraid when something drags behind him. Train him with a drag first. Drag training is basic to all pulling sports. At any time in your scooter career, you can go back to drag training to teach a concept or to increase strength.

Collect various items to be drags. Use quiet items such as a small branch with needles on it and noisy items such as tin cans. Mushers use tires. Start with a quiet, light weight drag. It can be leafy twigs, a burlap sack, or whatever you find. Attach the drag to the tug line and the tug line to the dog. Attach a long leash to his collar. Tell the dog to pull. You may have to walk beside him until he is at ease with the drag and will walk along calmly pulling it. Once he accepts the drag, drop behind him so that he and the drag are in front of you. Walk on down the trail behind the drag. Use treats liberally for a happy experience, if that is helpful.

Have the dog pull the drag over a variety of surfaces. Over grass it will have one sound and over gravel, a different sound. When the dog is at ease pulling the quiet drag, switch to a noisy drag like firewood. Work up to pulling tin cans on grass and then on pavement. Switch to a heavier drag like a tire. The dog will learn to put his head down and pull hard.

Harness vs collar: drag training teaches the dog to pull. It reinforces the concept that harnesses are for pulling and the collar is for walking without pulling. When the dog has learned to pull the drag, he is ready to pull the scooter. Follow the procedure for "The Dog Who Forges Ahead".

Training the Puppy to Pull

With a puppy, everything you do is training. The puppy has a lot to learn.

22. Millie, the pit bull, is pulling her tire. The leash to her collar is loose. Her tug line is tight. Photo of Millie and the author by Jessica Loveless, Alpine Outfitters, Roy, Washington.

- **Socialization**
  o how to get along with dogs
  o how to get along with cats
  o how to get along with people - adults, children and babies
  o how to understand language

- **Trust**
  o you will eat on time
  o you will sleep on time
  o you will be comfortable, pest free, and safe

- **Manners**
  o elimination
  o house manners
  o car manners

- **Mind and Body**
  o how to be an athlete (run, jump, balance, climb, turn, stop)

These days most puppies do not have the opportunity to run freely. They can't run the streets. Their yard is small. They have no play mates. They walk on leash in the parks. They grow up not really knowing how to use their back to run fast and powerfully. As much as possible, we puppy owners need to give our puppies active play and consistent socialization with people and other dogs.

by Daphne Lewis

Mushers provide plenty of supervised free running and free playing to their yearly crop of puppies. They turn their puppies loose once or twice a day into huge fenced paddocks. The mushers supervise the play. A few older dogs are turned into the pens with the puppies to speed around with them and to teach them manners. The puppies play tag. They run through and jump over culverts, climb on and walk along logs, play king-of-the-mountain on piles of dirt and keep-away with rope and sticks. They learn where their feet are and how to arch their backs to maximize speed.

The puppies also learn to follow the musher. The musher rides an ATV out of the play pen and his puppies run after him. They learn to traverse rough ground and avoid trees as they run after him for a few miles.

While it is hard for us city scooterers to duplicate this mental, social, and physical education for our puppies, we must try! In addition, we must give our future scooter dogs pulling education. We gage our lessons to the attention span of the puppy. Lessons are short - and easy.

Buy or sew a little harness for your puppy. Let him get used to wearing it. Once puppy wears his harness about the yard or house without thinking about it, put it on when you go for a walk. The harness means attention from the human; it means "I get to go outside and explore. My harness is good!" Take the harness off the puppy when you are not there to supervise. You do not want it to catch on something and neither do you want him to turn around and chew it.

Take puppy to a park or your back yard. Attach a line to his harness that will drag behind him. Play with him such that he forgets he is dragging a line. Once puppy is indifferent to pulling his line, you can attach a small branch to it and let him get used to dragging it around while exploring and playing. Leave this on only when you can supervise. You do not want him to get tangled or scared and you don't want him to turn around and bite the line in two.

23. Gracie, the pit bull puppy, pulls her leafy branch on her daily walk in Tacoma, Washington. Her owner, Cheryl Reehill of Liberty Dog Training, sewed the pink harness to use with puppies. Gracie walks confidently in front of Cheryl and pulls her drag easily. Gracie is three months old in this photo. Now a year later, Grace does weight pull and scootering with ease. She is never spooked by pulling things. Photo by author.

Leash your puppy. Let him walk in front of you. When he knows how to walk in front of you, let him walk in front of you while pulling his drag. My friend, Cheryl Reehill, goes for a walk with her puppy pulling a little branch of doug fir with its twigs and needles. Puppy pays no attention to harness, line or drag. Each day when Cheryl and Gracie go for a walk, Gracie wears her harness and pulls her little branch. Having a tug line behind her and a branch dragging on the ground is natural to her. She just goes about her puppy business of looking and listening and smelling as she walks. Whoo-eee, what a smart puppy.

Cheryl advises harness training a puppy soon after she arrives at your house. Cheryl put the harness on Gracie at seven weeks. For a puppy, learning to wear the harness is like learning to wear a collar. Cheryl does light dragging as soon as the pup is used to the harness. At four or five months she mostly continues walks with the pup pulling the drags but also does short scooter trips side by side with a quiet, mannerly older dog. At six to nine months the puppy pulls the scooter with the older dog two or three times a week for low mileage. Cheryl runs her puppy solo at a year. My pup was running solo (for short distances) at 7 months.

4) *The older puppy, leggy and full of energy.*

When puppies get to the age that they are too energetic with their barking, chewing, digging, and jumping, folks dump them at the animal shelter. In your case, you get a real harness to replace the puppy harness. Proceed to train as described above for an adult dog. Stop when the puppy wants more. The most important lesson is that pulling is fun. Still, it is good to tire them a little. "A tired puppy is a good puppy." A tired puppy sleeps and grows.

All dogs have an adult skeleton by two years. The growth plates even of giant dogs have finished growth by two years[2]. Breeders worry about puppies damaging the growth plates in their

24. Jill Miller's dog Scout helps her to train two siberian puppies. She ran him alone before running with the puppies so he would not run too fast for them. Photo courtesy of Jill Miller.

joints by exercising too much. Puppy owners listen carefully to the breeders. They become afraid to harness their puppies to a scooter before they are two years old. In contrast, common sense says that exercise in moderation is good for young dogs just as it is for young humans. Young bodies, minds and spirits develop better with plenty of exercise.

by Daphne Lewis

Mushers run their pups on teams beginning about six months of age. A couple of older, slower dogs lead the team and teach the pups. Puppy teams run slowly and for short distances. The pups learn to run on a team but they are never asked to pull hard or to run fast. They are not soured or frightened by their experience in harness because it is geared to their ability.

Professional mushers sometimes enter two teams in the long distance endurance races. Their best team is made up of experienced dogs between three and 10 years old. Their second team consists of yearlings. A helper runs the second team to give them experience. The yearlings are not expected to or asked to perform as well as the older dogs. Some mushers do not "work" their dogs until three years old. "Working" means training hard to win races where the dogs run 50 to 100 miles a day. "Working" means eight hours on and 6 hours off around the clock. No scooter dog is expected to work that hard whether young or old!

5) The dog who learns from other dogs.

Dogs learn quickly when hitched up beside another dog. It is a good idea to go through the basic training outlined above before hitching newbie beside your experienced dog. Many people can't wait, though, and hitch the two together right away. It generally works just fine. Be careful not to stress the new dog by going too far or too fast.

Recently I scootered behind Meeka, a dog who was obedience trained but had never scootered. We scootered in a group of eight people and dogs. Meeka did great. She kept up easily with the fastest dogs in the group. Later in the run, we hitched her with a deaf dog to teach him. You would never guess to see her that this was her first time pulling a scooter and that she had had no ground training.

Developing the Scooter Dog

You and your dog can scooter down the trail. It is fun. You are hooked. The dog gets excited when the harness comes out. It is time to train the commands.

PULL The Dog learned "Pull" (or "Let's go" or "hike") in the beginning lessons. Now refine the concept. Work with the dog until he pulls steadily without any reminder. Do not repeat a command. Train him to continue pulling at the appropriate pace until you tell him "Whoa", "Easy", or "Hike it up". Good mushers run along silently. Repeating commands is nagging. Amateurs nag.

---

[2] Lisa Nicolello, veterinarian technician, Gold Coast Mastiffs, by e-mail 2004.

GEE & HAW These commands can be taught while walking on leash, pulling a drag, sitting in the living room with a clicker, or while scootering.

Your dog is trotting down the trail while you ride the scooter. A fork appears. You say "Gee". If the dog turns to the right, his reward is to continue going and of course your enthusiastic, "Good dog! Good gee!". If the dog turns left, put on the brakes and say nothing. The dog will try turning right. Release the brakes; say "Good Dog. Good gee" and continue down the trail. The reward for the correct decision is to continue going.

Some scooterers teach gee and haw on the trail by throwing a treat in the appropriate direction. Later chucking a rock serves to remind the dogs. When skijoring, chucking a snowball in the right direction gives the cue. The dogs pick up on motion[3].

CJ Schuyler taught gee and haw with a clicker in the living room.

Hi Lacey,

I taught the turns by starting in my living room with a clicker. I sat on the couch with the dog's rear facing me as it stood between my knees. I'd say Gee as I was holding a treat to my right and when the dog looked to the right I'd click and treat. After a few times I'd wait to hold the treat out until the dog looked to the right. Once it looked in that direction I'd click and treat (C/T). After two days of them just looking to the right I held the treat out far enough that when they looked right they also had to take a step to the right. This became the Gee (look and step right). Once they had this down I didn't try to keep them between my knees. They understood that Gee meant look and step to the right. I only did Gee for the first week and then started over with Haw. Once gee/haw were understood at that level I put their harness on (still working in the living room) and asked for a line out on a 6 foot leash. Then, while they were lining out I'd say Gee, wait for them to look and step once to the right. I'd click and toss the treat to their right as the reward. Did this to the left as well and both lead dogs now have an excellent gee/haw. I should go back and do this with the rest of the dogs but I am doing it the easy way by letting the trained dogs teach the others. I am not too worried about the learning curve for the rest of the dogs since my two lead dogs are great gee/haw dogs. - CJ[4]

GO STRAIGHT - Use the same techniques as for gee and haw.

One scooterer taught these commands with ground training. He mowed a large circle in his back meadow. He mowed a path across the diameter of the circle (the Y axis) and a path perpendicular to it (the X axis). He walked the dog on leash up the Y axis of the circle. When he came to the intersection of the X axis, he commanded "Go Straight". Since Gypsy was on leash, it was easy to have her go straight. When the two of them arrived at the circumference, he could teach either gee or haw. When he got his scooter, he practiced turns while scootering on the mowed paths.

COME HAW - This is another command that can be taught with ground training, drag training or while scootering.

---

[3] Megan Capon, e-mail report, 2004.
[4] e-mail to DogsLovetoRun@yahoogroups.com, November, 2004

by Daphne Lewis

ON BY - "On by" is a command specific to mushing. To teach it, you need an assistant. Station your assistant somewhere not too far away from you. Walk the dog on leash towards the assistant. As you get close, say to the dog, "Go say Hi". Let the dog go over and get petted. Continue walking. Circle back and pass by the assistant again. Say "Go say hi" again. The third time around, change the command to "On by". Walk briskly past the assistant, taking the dog with you. Do this exercise a few more times varying the command. You can do this exercise with the tug line attached to both collar and harness. You pull on the harness with your left hand and guide via the collar with your right hand.

An excellent way to train "On by" is with a group. A group of 10 or so people with their dogs sitting beside them make a big open circle. One person with his dog walks around the circle weaving in and out between the people and seated dogs. The tug line is snapped both to collar and harness as in ground training. The dog is told "On by" and praised when he walks by the seated dogs. He is corrected if he veers towards them. The dogs in the circle sitting beside their owners are also learning "on by". They are to ignore the dog and human walking past them.

When the first team returns to its place in the circle, the next team starts. When all 10 teams have had their turn, the first team starts again but weaving in the opposite direction. This exercise can be done a couple of times.

To teach On By when passing head on, the group forms two lines about 50 feet apart. The two lines walk towards each other, cross in the middle and continue to the other side. Dogs are corrected if they swerve or turn their heads towards another dog. No "evil eyes" are permitted.

"On by" training continues when you are on scootering runs. As you approach a distraction such as a person walking a dog on a leash, remind your dog to "On by". Be ready to enforce the command. Enforcing it may mean using a more forceful voice or jumping off the scooter, grabbing the collar and running beside the dog while pushing the scooter past the distraction. The trained scooter dog will assume that he is to go on by all distractions unless told otherwise.

Pedestrians walking their dogs are surprised by someone telling their dog to ignore and go on by. They are accustomed to letting dogs say hello and sniff.

Which brings up sniffing and peeing on bushes. Perhaps in spite of your training efforts your dog veers off the trail to sniff. I believe that for most dogs the ground training just described will work. However many a scooterer has yelled out "No! Leave it! ON BY!" In time just "On by" said calmly will suffice. One of the finest sled dog trainers I know trained her male to stop sniffing and peeing in a different and very effective way. When her enthusiastic young dog veered to the side of the trail, the tire of the scooter ran into him. "Oh, I am so sorry, Rogan, imagine that. You stopped and the tire ran into you." This accident that he caused "happened" one more time. Rogan stopped sniffing and peeing. Of course as trainer, you have to be careful that the tire does not hurt the dog when it "accidentally" rolls into him. And you have to know, that the dog adores scootering and the scooter before letting a tire roll near him.

PASSING

Passing another scooterer or a musher is a refinement of "on by". It is best to go out with another team, pass once and continue going. Passing and repassing the same team is leap frogging and that is not what wins the race.

READY

Use this when first starting out and after rest breaks along the trail. It is fun to see the dog get up from his rest and get ready to go again.

HIKE, HIKE IT UP and EASY

Many scooterers use "Hike" for "Start pulling", and, "Hike it up" for "Move faster". They use "Easy" for "Move slower". "Easy" and "Hike it Up" are relative to the speed the dog is going. If the dog is walking, "Hike it up" may mean "Trot". The excitement in your voice colors the meaning of the command. If the dog is racing along at a run and you say "Easy", he will drop into a fast lope. Say "Easy" again and he will drop into a slow lope or fast trot.

You can work on change of pace with leash walking. Use the words "Easy" and "Hike it up" as you walk, jog and run. Change pace gradually and use the words as you change pace.

To work on change of pace while scootering, use your brakes. Give the command "Easy". If the dog slows down, "Good Dog. Good easy." If the dog ignores "Easy", squeeze and release the brakes. In other words pulse the brakes. If the dog slows down, "Good dog. Good easy". If he speeds up again, pulse the brakes again but don't repeat the command. He should learn to maintain a given speed until told otherwise.

Some dogs dislike slowing down. Try pulsing the brakes and having them slow down for just a few seconds. Then tell them to speed up again. Gradually increase the amount of time that they will hold the slower pace. Reward them with allowing them to run again.

"Easy" is important. Some dogs start out at top speed for the first mile or two until they run out of steam. If you train the dog to start at a sustainable speed, he will be able to run greater distances. He will have the resilience at the end of a race or fun run to speed up for the last half mile before the finish line or car.

Easy is also important when running several dogs. You need to slow the faster dogs so the slower ones can keep up. Slowing the faster ones with training and braking allows you to praise the slower ones for catching up and keeping their tug lines tight.

by Daphne Lewis

To teach "Hike it up", put excitement into your voice. "Go, go, go, go!" worked for Millie and me. Kick like crazy to make the scooter easy to pull and the dog may take off running faster and faster. Fun!

WALK

"Walk" allows you to walk beside the scooter while the dog walks in front of you pulling the scooter. Walk is a useful command when:

- on a crowded sidewalk,
- crossing a street in a cross walk,
- pulling a wheel chair or a wagon,
- the dog needs to cool down,
- the hill is steep and you are out of breath,
- climbing or descending stairs,
- crossing lawns that say "no bicycles",
- navigating sticky muddy trails,
- navigating a single track trail full of low branches and roots,
- sharing a trail with horses,
- scootering with an injured dog,
- pushing a scooter with a flat tire.

WHOA or WAIT

These words are easily taught in the house, on leash, and during ground training.

When scootering, say the word once. Enforce it with the brakes and of course with ample praise.

25. Dulcie and Rogan, german short hair pointers, line out awaiting the command to go. Photo by Megan Capon, the skier attached to the tug line.

LINE OUT

This command is specific to all mushing dogs, including scooter dogs. When you attach a novice dog to the scooter, you lay the scooter on its side with tug line attached and stretched forward full length. You don't use the kick stand because the scooter will fall when the dog lines out. You bring the harnessed dog to the outstretched tug line and snap it to his harness. You tell the dog to stay and you walk back to the scooter. The dog ignores "Stay" and follows you back to the scooter. His tug line tangles about his legs and under his belly. You untangle him and walk him by the collar back to the front of the scooter and tell him to stay. You snap the tug line again to his harness. You rush back to the scooter to pick it up before he has a chance to break his stay. He follows you back again. You decide that teaching "line out" is a good idea and you marvel at the training it takes to run 16 dogs on a sled - let alone from Anchorage to Nome.

To teach "Line out", snap the scooter end of the tug line to a fence or anything that won't move. If you secure the scooter to the fence, and snap the tugline to it, the training is more realistic. Bring the harnessed dog on leash to the tug line and snap it to his harness. Tell the dog "Line out" and coax him towards you by word and leash until the tug line is stretched tight. Tell him,"Good dog. Good line out". Proof him. Walk a few steps to one side. Should he hold position, "Good dog". Walk to the other side. Should he shift his body to watch you, use the leash to place him back in line-out position. He is welcome to move his head to watch you. He must keep the line tight, however. When he has stayed in line out position as you walk from side to side, walk behind him. Continue the praise and corrections as needed. Drop the leash and walk behind and around. The dog should hold the line out position no matter where you are.

You can teach line out with the scooter attached to the immovable object. Attach the tug line from the scooter to the dog. Practice line out until the dog is expert. Use treats and/or clicker training if you want. Line out is especially important when you have more than one dog pulling the scooter.

The dog is performing line out whenever he is harnessed to the scooter. When he is standing, he is facing away

25. Dogs learn "line out" at a pull clinic given by Cascade Sled Dog Club in Oregon, 2004. Photo by Jessica Loveless, Alpine Outfitters, Roy, Washington.

from the scooter holding the line tight. When he is trotting, he is facing away from the scooter holding the line tight. Moving or standing, he is performing line out when attached to the scooter.

You as scooter rider must assist the dog in lining out. Use the brakes to hold the scooter back and the line tight whenever the scooter begins to catch up with the dog, especially when going down hill. The dog counts on pressure on the harness. If you let the scooter go faster and relieve the pressure, the dog is caught off guard. He can injure himself - like you slipping on a patch of ice. Use the brakes to keep pressure on the line when going downhill. Let your dog go fast on level ground but keep speeds moderate or even slow going downhill. Going down hill is a good time to let the dog rest (think interval training). Regain speed when you are on level ground again.

Do not let the scooter catch up with the dog. If your children run your dog, emphasize this point, "Do not pass the family dog when going downhill!"

Once your dog loves to scooter, he will be impatient to start running. Use his desire to run to reinforce "Line out". He must stand still without barking and shrieking before he can run. Vary the amount of time at line out before beginning each run.

Conditioning

Weight

Chris Zinc, DVM, Ph.D., writes the following in "Corpulent Canines?", an article I saw on her web site in 2004. "I have assessed the weight on hundreds of dogs of a variety of breeds over the past year at seminars all over the country and a conservative estimate is that about 50% of the dogs that I see are overweight; approximately 25% are actually obese."

As coach for your dog, you must maintain him at the best weight for running. A dog is overweight if he is shaped like a hot dog with no indentation at the waist as you look down on him. He is overweight if you can't feel his ribs when you run your hand over them. With most dogs you should see the outline of the ribs closest to his hips. With dogs with little coat, you may be able to see most of the ribs. With very hairy dogs, the ribs are hidden but they can be felt. Seeing the ribs <u>slightly</u> is the goal. You do not want a dog so thin that the ribs stick out.

Most dogs have a tuck up behind their ribs at their waist. Some breeds such as bull terriers are shown in conformation with little or no tuckup. They have a rather straight line from chest to rear knee so as to appear barrel chested and strong. It is fat that swells the abdomen and reduces the tuck up. It is not muscle. It is not fitness and strength. Once your dog has won his ribbons in conformation, remove those extra 10 or 20 pounds. Change his appearance from round bodied show dog to lean bodied athlete. Your lean dog will run better. He will live longer. His joints will endure less wear and tear. He will also look better!

Food

Feeding the athletic dog is an art. Look critically at the dog and perhaps feel his ribs as you decide how much to feed him each day.

I know healthy dogs who are fed kibble. Some of the top mushers feed kibble only. Others feed kibble with extra meat and fat during heavy training and racing. I also know healthy dogs who are fed raw food. Feed what you think best. If you feed kibble, feed brands where meat is the first and main ingredient, not corn or wheat. Dogs do not do well eating grains. Supplement kibble with raw treats because raw food has enzymes and vitamins that are destroyed by cooking. If you feed raw, feed the meat and bones as they come, ie., the whole chicken wing with its skin and bones and meat, or the whole back or the whole half bird. The meat is full of phosphorus and the bones are full of calcium. Meat alone is an unbalanced food. Read on the many web sites about how to feed a raw diet. Cooked poultry bones become brittle and dangerous. Raw ones are fine for dogs.

A raw beef knuckle bone gives hours of happy chewing. Chewing a bone alleviates boredom. Bones scrape tartar off teeth and massage gums to keep them healthy. Bones are fattening. Reduce the dog's regular food on the days you give a beef bone. Raw eggs given unbroken in the shell taste terrific and the shells are full of calcium. Chicken necks are cheap and dogs love to eat them. I feed raw food because it is natural for a canine. My eleven-year-old rottweiler has a glossy coat, good health and good gums. His lameness comes from accidents, not from old age.

27. Rubro, age eleven.

Supplements

Years ago my vet told me to supplement my rottweiler's food with vitamins C and E and essential fatty acids. I think he looks young for an eleven-year-old rottweiler. You can buy tablets of essential fatty acids or bottles of oil from your vet. You also can buy salmon oil in a bottle at pet stores and flaxseed oil at health stores. Mix one part of each with 2 parts of olive oil and you have a healthy way to flavor ground raw vegetables and to supplement kibble. For simplicity, I give fish oil tablets from Costco. I have to wrap them in sandwich meat or he spits them out.

by Daphne Lewis

Water

Mushers give their dogs water an hour or two before a run. They want the dog to be well hydrated during his run but they don't want his stomach weighted with water. Often they bait the water to be sure the dog drinks it. Baiting water means adding flavoring so the dogs enjoy drinking it. They also give baited water after a run. They wait for the heavy panting to die down and then offer the water. Dog outfitters sell powders to mix with the water. The powders taste great to the dog and speed their recovery from lactic acid build up.

We carry water in fanny packs or handlebar bags on our scooter fun runs in western Washington. We stop often to rest the dogs and to wait for stragglers. We offer water at most rest stops. Most of the time, the dogs want to drink after ten minutes of running. However, now that we know to give lots of water two hours before the run, the dogs are not drinking the water we carry. They are not thirsty.

Heat

Dogs do not cool as efficiently as humans and horses. They evaporate water from their tongues and the bottoms of their feet rather than from their entire skin. Dogs can overheat and die of heat stroke. If your dog overheats, cool him immediately by what ever means you have. Get him out of the sun. Immerse him in water in a ditch, pond, or stream. If these are not available, stick his feet in a water bowl. Douse his ear leather. Squirt water from your water bottle down his throat. Rub it into his fur down to his skin. Once a dog overheats, he remains sensitive to heat thereafter. You may have to get him to a vet pronto.

Always consider the weather when scootering. In Florida scooterers and mushers train at night to beat the heat. Some people train at 1 am. Sled dogs acclimated to Alaska weather are hot at 50 degrees. Dogs acclimated to southern California consider 50 degrees to be cool weather. Dogs used to warm weather, can run at temperatures that northern dogs could not withstand. Dogs running in warm weather run more slowly than the same dogs in cold temperatures.

If you run your dogs in

28. Two huskies trot through live oaks, pines, and palmettos in Florida. At 70 degrees Fahrenheit, it is too hot for running but OK for leisurely trotting by acclimated dogs. The rider is the photographer's nine year old son, Charles. The beach is 300 feet away so rapid cooling is possible. Photo by Dominic Gaudin.

warm weather, choose a route where they can swim along the way. On our Fun Runs in Seattle, we stop to rest as soon as the dogs' tongues hang far out. We rest in the shade, give the dogs water to drink and maybe wet down their heads. We wait until the tongues shorten back up before running again. Generally a few dogs start acting playful and that is a cue to start again.

When the weather cools down in fall, dogs get excited. They run faster and farther. Winter becomes a favorite season for people who run dogs. They even wish that summer were over, an unthinkable thought before they began running dogs! Before running dogs, we wished for summer; after running dogs, we wish for winter.

Coaching

You, the coach, set goals. What will your goals be?

Breeders scooter to build fitness so the dog wins in the show ring. Hunters scooter to build endurance for stunning performance in the field. Skijorers scooter to build speed to win races. Agility competitors scooter to build fitness without continual jumping. Scooterers scooter because they love exploring trails with their dogs.

I assume that before long a dog scooter association will form. It will sponsor Scooter Dog titles and scooter races. Your goal could be to title the dog in scootering or it could be to win races. My goal for my new puppy, a presa canario, will be to build fitness. We can explore mountains, forests and beaches in Washington State. I dream of someday scootering the great trails: the Appalachian Trail and the Pacific Crest Trail. A goal for retirement!

What is possible?

Dogs are remarkable athletes. Sprint dogs bred by top mushers and trained with skill, complete 20 mile races in just over an hour. These dogs can be coached to run fast for 20 miles or to run moderately for 100 miles. The dog's training determines his status as sprint runner or distance runner. Distance dogs reserve energy for the long haul. Sprint racers do not. It is possible to turn a sprint dog into a distance dog. It is difficult to turn a distance dog into a sprint dog because the distance dog keeps a reserve.

With scooter dogs, reserving energy comes with experience. You will find that older dogs keep their reserve. Younger dogs blast away without holding back. Dogs who frequently go on 10 or 20 mile weekend runs are more apt to reserve energy than dogs who rarely go more than 2 miles.

by Daphne Lewis

Times of Sled Dog

Teams	Average Speed	Winning Speed
3-dog Class - 3-4 miles	15 mph	18 mph
6-Dog Class - 6-8 miles	15 mph	22 mph
8-Dog Class - 8-10 miles	18 mph	28 mph

Coaching

Coaching a scooter dog is like coaching yourself. You run a little farther each run. You allow enough rest between runs for your muscles to recover. After you can run the distance you are training for, you do interval training. You alternate between jogging and running. It is the same for a scooter dog.

Some dogs start their scooter runs at breakneck speed. Consider turning them into sprint dogs. Instead of working to teach them to start out at a 10 mile an hour trot, increase their ability to maintain speed. Do interval training. Notice when your headstrong runner is about to slow down. Perhaps after three minutes, your dog is tiring. Stop quickly before he slows down. Rest with him for three minutes. Then sprint again for three minutes. Rest another three minutes. Tell him 'easy' and trot back to the car. The next day is a rest and recover day. You may do some drag training with a tire to build strength but you won't sprint. The third day you work again at speed. Your dog is not tiring at three minutes so you stop him at five minutes and rest for five minutes. The second sprint may be four minutes and you may be able to sprint a third time. Or not. The idea is increase the time he can maintain good speed. As he gets stronger he also may increase his top speed. Stop just before the dog starts to slow. Rest an equal number of minutes as the dog sprinted.

Some sprint mushers never allow their dogs to trot. The dogs run or lope. Rests occur by stopping not by trotting. This training is appropriate for leggy lightweight dogs. Many of the heavier breeds trot more easily than they lope.

29. A german shorthair pointer and a youth race in Europe. The driver wears a helmet and gloves. Photo courtesy of Filip Chludil of Czechoslovakia. Filip Chludil of Czechoslovakia.

Most scooterers are not sprint racers. They need a range of speeds. For the dog to start off his run at top speed out of the driveway and on to the sidewalk is not useful. They want controlled speed, not wild abandon.

Some dogs are difficult to slow down at the start of a run. If you apply the brakes to slow them, they just hammer the harness and may even tear up their pads. With these dogs, run on a trail where speed is OK for the first mile. After that first rush you can train a sustainable lope or a fast trot.

Most people scootering with their dogs do not have races available within reasonable distance. Many do not have dogs who want to run flat out. These dogs prefer to trot. Their coaching goal would be different. Maybe they train to go on trails in the wild lands for ten or twenty miles on weekends. They coach for distance rather than for speed. They gradually increase distance. Say the first few weeks, they go for a mile each run. When this becomes easy, add another half mile. Drop back to one mile a few times. Then do the mile and a half several times until that also becomes easy. As you build up mileage, mix short fast runs along with longer, endurance runs. You add mileage when the dog can do the distance without walking.

Once the dog can run the distance that you are aiming for, say an hour on a Sunday morning, you can work on speed. If an occasion arises where you want to go several hours on a weekend, you can do it. Run for the normal hour and then take a break until the dog is eager to go again. Common sense again. From your own experience you know that if you walk for 50 minutes every other day, you can hike over the weekend for hours.

Mushers do not kick/scoot to help their dogs. The dogs learn to pull harder when it becomes more difficult rather than turning around and looking pathetically towards the musher. The exception to the do-not-help rule is running up hills. If a team charges up hills, it can pick up speed over a team that slows down and walks up hills. Mushers use ATV's to train their teams because the ATV is heavy enough to control a big team. They will keep the machine in gear on the flats and downhill to increase the drag. However, when a hill comes, they may use the engine to release drag. Feeling no weight, the dogs bound up the hill. Hill charging becomes a habit that transfers to pulling a sled - and winning races.

Be flexible in your coaching plans. Sometimes you plan a long run and the dogs are having a bad day. Change your plans. Turn around sooner than you planned. Do a little whoa and down/stay training. Practice line out. Throw the ball for the dog or let him swim in a lake. When you scooter back to the car, great snacks are waiting - (as always!). Or maybe you planned to work on interval training for speed development. The dogs are sluggish. You change plans. Perhaps you still run the route you planned but you work on controlled trotting instead of fast running. You work with the command 'Easy'.

by Daphne Lewis

End the run on a positive note. Jim Tofflemire, retired Iditarod musher in Oregon, says, "Continually evaluate, adapt, and adjust. Because we are dealing with living beings, it's a constantly moving target we are aiming for."

Mushers are careful to note when a dog loses enthusiasm or is not quite up to his usual performance. They don't assume the dog has developed a bad attitude. They look for a physical cause. A small injury such as a tear in a pad or a pulled muscle can explain a dog's reluctance. They are quick to massage sore muscles. Time off heals injuries and restores the dog's eagerness to run.

How will the sport develop?

Dog sports can become popular very quickly. Agility is an excellent example. It was invented in 1987 as entertainment between events at Crufts Dog Show in London, England. Clubs sprang up quickly around the world. They organized local, regional, national and international competitions. As popularity rose, dog magazines ran articles describing the sport. Small businesses sprang up to make equipment. People became hooked on the sport and chose their next dog from a breed that excels at agility.

Dog scootering is a new sport (in the United States) the way agility was less than twenty years ago. Dog scootering will follow the same pattern of development. It will become well known among dog people. It will be obvious to consider dog scootering when wondering what activity to do with your dog. A dog scooter association will form. It will develop rules for events and by-laws for clubs. It will provide assistance in the form of rules for events and by-laws for nonprofit status.

I think that canicross is another dry land sport that will increase in popularity as will driving in a sulky. Athletes in wheel chairs would enjoy traveling and racing with their service/mobility dogs.

At the time of writing this book at the close of 2005, encouraging events have happened.

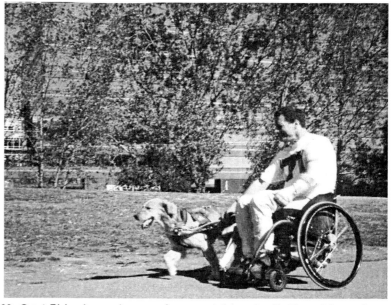
30. Grant Richardson enjoys an afternoon at the park with his assistance dog, Joey. Joey can pull the chair while trotting beside it thanks to a custom harness by Alpine Outfitters. Photo by author.

1. Mushers now consider a scooter a normal part of their training equipment.
2. An e-mail list for dog scooterers, **DogsLovetoRun@yahoogroups.com**, has 533 members, and a new one for southern scooterers has begun.
3. Scooter manufacturers realize that dog owners are potential customers. Some mention dog scootering on their web sites.

by Daphne Lewis

4. The web site DogScooter.com is specific to the sport. It gets 50,000 hits a year.
5. Alpine Outfitters designed a harness specifically for dog scootering.
6. The International Federation of Sleddog Sports (IFSS) included scootering in the world championship races scheduled in Nov. 2002 and 2003 and February 2005.

31. The author enjoys driving with eleven month old Tess on a bike trail in Redmond, Washington. The sulky has a dorsal hitch instead of the usual two shafts plus traces. It has disk brakes and independently suspended wheels. It is fast, easy to pull, and fun to drive. Tess knows gee and haw and responds quickly to the reins attached to the two D rings in her driving collar. Tess is a presa canario. Her long legs and powerful body make her an ideal driving dog.

Meanwhile, dog owners are scootering with their dogs. They are not waiting for the clubs to form. Their golden retrievers are pulling them around the lake. Their deaf dog is running beside their hearing dog. They are adopting a small dog to pull their son while their larger dog pulls them. They are going to the store via dog scooter. They are heading into back country and meeting skunks, porcupines and deer.

People dog scooter to enjoy their dog. They also do it to enjoy scenery, save on gasoline, get their mind off work, and enjoy the compliments of passersby. One of these days, dog scooterers will commute by a combination of dog scooter and public transportation. They and their dog will scooter to the bus stop, hop on the bus, crate the dog in the office, walk him at lunch, recrate him for the afternoon, get on the bus, get off the bus and dog scooter home.